READING COMPREHENSION HIGH SCHOOL

READING COMPREHENSION GRADE 9-12 WORKBOOK: ACHIEVE HIGHER TEST SCORES WITH INTERACTIVE EXERCISES

DR. FANATOMY

copyright@ dr. fanatomy 2024

All rights reserved. No part of this publication may be reproduced, distributed, or transmitted in any form or by any means, including photocopying, recording, or other electronic or mechanical methods, without the prior written permission of the publisher, except in the case of brief quotations embodied in critical reviews and certain other noncommercial uses permitted by copyright law.

This book is a work of non-fiction, and any resemblance to actual persons, living or dead, or actual events is purely coincidental.

The information and techniques described in this book are intended for educational and informational purposes only. The author and publisher shall not be held liable for any injury, damage, or loss arising from using or misusing the information presented in this book.

While every effort has been made to ensure the accuracy of the information contained within this book, the author and publisher make no warranties or representations express or implied, about the completeness, accuracy, reliability, suitability, or availability with respect to the contents of this book for any purpose. The use of any information provided in this book is at the reader's own risk.

Bonus Booklet For You!

With great pleasure, I warmly welcome you to purchase the book. Congratulations on stepping towards improving yourself and developing the skills necessary to thrive as a teenager and beyond.

Below is a surprise gift for you!

Download it from the link (or scan the QR code below)
https://bit.ly/TeeNavigationBonus

TABLE OF CONTENTS

1. INTRODUCTION TO READING COMPREHENSION (Pg:4-9)

- Welcome Message
- Definition
- Levels of Comprehension
- Practical Example
- Importance of Reading in Everyday Life
- Types of Reading: Fiction, Non-Fiction, Technical, and Literary Texts
- Trivia Corner
- Activity Corner 1

2. UNDERSTANDING THE MAIN IDEA (Pg:10-15)

- What is the Main Idea?
- Differentiating Between the Main Idea and Supporting Details
- Strategies to Identify the Main Idea
- Practical Example: Finding the Main Idea in a News Article
- Read a Short Passage and Identify the Main Idea
- Trivia Corner
- Activity Corner 2

3. RECOGNIZING SUPPORTING DETAILS (Pg:16-22)

- What are the Supporting Details?
- How to Locate Supporting Information in a Text
- Importance of Supporting Details in Strengthening Arguments
- Practical Example: Analyzing a Persuasive Essay for Supporting Details
- Exercise: Highlight Supporting Details in a Given Passage
- Supporting Details Often Double as Evidence to Convince the Reader
- Trivia Corner
- Activity Corner 3

4. INFERENCE AND INTERPRETATION SKILLS (Pg:23-29)

- What is an Inference?
- How to Make Logical Inferences from the Text
- Key Interpretation Strategies for Complex Texts
- Practical Example: Making Inferences from a Mystery Story
- Exercise: Infer the Meaning of a Paragraph Based on Contextual Clues
- Trivia Corner
- Activity Corner 4

5. ANALYZING THE AUTHOR'S PURPOSE AND TONE (Pg: 30-39)

- Understanding Author's Purpose
- Examples of Author's Purpose
- Recognizing Tone
- Practical Example: Identifying Tone in Political Speeches and Articles
- Exercise: Determine the Author's Purpose and Tone in a Passage
- Trivia: How an Author's Background Influences Their Tone
- 10 examples of purpose and tone
- Trivia Corner
- Activity Corner 5

6. VOCABULARY IN CONTEXT (Pg: 40-46)

- Why Vocabulary Matters in Reading Comprehension
- Practical Example
- Readers Exposed to a Rich Vocabulary Are 60% More Likely to Comprehend Complex Texts.
- Fascinating Origins of Everyday Words
- Trivia Corner
- Activity Corner 6

7. IDENTIFYING TEXT STRUCTURE (Pg: 47-53)

- Introduction
- Benefits of Text Structure in Reading
- Practical Example: Identifying the Structure in a Historical Document
- Exercise: Label the Text Structure in a Paragraph
- Trivia Corner
- Activity Corner 7

8. SUMMARIZING AND PARAPHRASING (Pg: 54-61)

- The Art of Summarizing
- Key Elements of Summarizing
- Practical Example: Summarizing a Chapter of a Popular Book
- Paraphrasing: Retelling in Your Own Words
- Practical Example: Paraphrasing a Passage
- Practical Example: Summarizing a Chapter of a Popular Book
- Summarizing Boosts Information Retention
- Final Thoughts
- Trivia Corner
- Activity Corner 8

9. READING BEYOND THE TEXT: CRITICAL THINKING AND REFLECTION
(Pg: 62-71)

- *Reading with a Critical Eye*
- *Key Elements of Summarizing*
- *Example of Critical Reading in Action*
- *Critical Reading Response*
- *Asking Deeper Questions*
- *Reflecting on the Text: Connecting with Personal Experiences*
- *Practical Example: Critically Analyzing a Newspaper Editorial*
- *Critical Analysis Questions:*
- *Write a Reflection on a Chosen Article or Book Chapter:*
- *Trivia Corner*
- *Activity Corner 9*

ACTIVITY ANSWERS
(Pg: 82 -90)

CONCLUSION: YOUR JOURNEY TO MASTERING READING COMPREHENSION
(Pg: 91-92)

APPENDIX
(Pg: 93 - 96)

- *Appendix -A: Common Reading Comprehension Strategies*
- *Appendix -B: Reading Comprehension Question Types*
- *Appendix -C: Tips for Test-Taking*
- *Appendix - D: Glossary of Reading Comprehension Terms*
- *Appendix - E : Common Reading Comprehension Errors*

1. Introduction to Reading Comprehension

Welcome Message

Welcome to *"Reading Comprehension High School: Achieve Higher Test Scores with Interactive Exercises: Reading Comprehension Grade 9-12 workbook ."* This workbook is designed to help you improve your reading and comprehension skills, essential for academic success and effective communication. We are thrilled to be on this journey with you, offering expert guidance and interactive exercises to make learning engaging and impactful. Let's dive in and begin building a solid foundation for your future achievements!

Definition:

Reading comprehension involves understanding, interpreting, and analyzing written texts; it's about reading words and grasping their meaning, purpose, and connections.

Levels of Comprehension

Level	Description	Example
Literal	Understanding the basic meaning of the text	Recalling facts like dates or names from a news article
Inferential	Reading between the lines and making logical guesses	Guessing a character's emotions from their actions
Critical	Evaluating and analyzing the text for deeper meaning	Questioning an author's opinion or identifying bias
Creative	Applying the ideas from the text to new contexts or personal life	Using an idea from a novel to solve a real-world problem

Practical Example:

Detective Marlowe discovers a half-burned letter at the crime scene and a broken watch that stopped at exactly 10:15 PM. These clues help establish the timeline of the murder. However, the suspect had an alibi for that time but was seen leaving the scene at 10:45 PM, suggesting the watch may have been tampered with to frame someone else. As the reader critically examines the case, they might question whether the broken watch was a red herring designed to mislead the detective and the audience. In a creative twist, the reader could imagine that the real culprit was a character who had only been briefly mentioned earlier, reshaping the entire ending of the mystery.

Comprehension Type	Explanation	Example from Paragraph
Literal Comprehension	Understanding and remembering the key facts and clues presented in the story.	Detective Marlowe finds a half-burned letter and a broken watch stopped at 10:15 PM, which establishes the timeline.
Inferential Comprehension	Using the clues to make logical conclusions or predictions beyond what is explicitly stated.	The reader infers that the watch may have been tampered with since the suspect had an alibi but was seen leaving later.
Critical Comprehension	Evaluating the fairness, logic, and validity of the clues and their purpose in the story.	The reader questions whether the broken watch was a deliberate red herring meant to mislead both the detective and the audience.
Creative Comprehension	Expanding the narrative by imagining alternate scenarios, twists, or conclusions.	The reader imagines that the real culprit was a character briefly mentioned earlier, changing the mystery's outcome.

Importance of Reading in Everyday Life:

Relevance to Teens:

Reading isn't just about school. You read social media posts, news articles, song lyrics, game guides, and more every day. Comprehending what you read helps you navigate life better, whether understanding complex instructions, making informed decisions, or simply enjoying a good story.

Benefits of Reading in Real-Life Scenarios

Scenario	How Reading Helps	Example
Social Media	Understanding tone and intention in posts and comments	Avoiding misunderstandings in text conversations
News Articles	Identifying reliable information and fake news	Knowing when an article is biased or misleading
Text Messages	Interpreting emotion and meaning from short texts	Knowing when a friend is being sarcastic or serious
Job Applications	Understanding job descriptions and crafting thoughtful responses	Tailoring your resume and cover letter to specific roles
Gaming Guides	Following instructions to improve gameplay	Mastering new skills in games like Fortnite or Minecraft

Reading enhances cognitive function and boosts critical thinking skills, which is essential for strategic gaming and career readiness.

Types of Reading: Fiction, Non-Fiction, Technical, and Literary Texts

Different types of reading materials require distinct approaches. Whether losing oneself in a fantasy novel or absorbing information from a science textbook, the engagement with texts varies based on their purpose.

Type of Reading	Purpose	Example	Approach
Fiction	Entertainment, imagination	Reading a fantasy novel like Harry Potter	Focus on plot, characters, and themes
Non-Fiction	Information, learning	Reading a biography of a historical figure	Look for facts, key events, and the author's point of view
Technical	Practical, instructional	Reading a manual for building a model or fixing a computer	Pay attention to details and step-by-step processes
Literary	Deep analysis and interpretation	Reading classic literature like To Kill a Mockingbird	Focus on themes, symbolism, and character development

Practical Example

Say you're reading a technical guide to learn how to build a gaming PC. You must carefully follow the step-by-step instructions and understand the technical terms like "GPU" and "motherboard." When reading fiction, like a dystopian novel (The Hunger Games), you'll focus on the characters' emotions, relationships, and world.

Identify Types of Reading Materials

Below are short excerpts from different types of texts. Could you identify whether the excerpt is Fiction, Non-Fiction, Technical, or Literary?

a) "The CPU, or Central Processing Unit, is the computer's brain, responsible for executing instructions." - *Technical*
b) "As Katniss entered the arena, her heart raced, but her mind was focused on survival." - *Fiction*
c) "In 1969, Neil Armstrong became the first person to walk on the moon, marking a historic moment for humanity."- *Non-Fiction*
d) "The scarlet letter burned on her chest, symbolizing shame and defiance against society."- Literary

Trivia Corner

- The average person reads between 200-300 words per minute, but speed readers can read up to 1,000 words per minute!

- Your brain processes visuals 60,000 times faster than text, so we often look at pictures or videos before reading.

- Students who read for fun regularly tend to score higher on standardized tests like the SAT and ACT.

 ACTIVITY CORNER 1
Introduction to Reading Comprehension

1. Identify the Reading Type

Instructions: Below are excerpts from different types of reading materials. Identify whether the text is Fiction, Non-Fiction, Technical, or Literary.

1. "Neil Armstrong took his first step on the moon in 1969, saying, 'That's one small step for man, one giant leap for mankind.'"
2. "Harry stared at the letter, his heart pounding. He was accepted into Hogwarts!"
3. "Insert the USB drive into the port on your computer, ensuring the correct orientation. Next, click on 'My Computer' to locate the device."
4. "The scarlet letter burned brightly against her chest, a permanent reminder of her shame and defiance."
5. "Photosynthesis is the process by which plants convert sunlight into energy."

2. Match the Reading Purpose

Instructions: Match each type of reading with its primary purpose.

Type of Reading	Purpose
1. Fiction	a) Provides step-by-step instructions
2. Non-Fiction	b) Explores complex themes through deep analysis
3. Technical	c) Conveys factual information
4. Literary	d) Tells a story or sparks imagination

2. Understanding the Main Idea

What is the Main Idea?

The main idea is the central point or message that the author is trying to convey in a passage or text. It's the big picture around which the details revolve.

Main Idea vs. Supporting Details

Component	Description	Example
Main Idea	The primary message or point of the passage	Recycling reduces environmental pollution.
Supporting Details	Specific information that explains or reinforces the main idea	Recycling plastic saves energy and reduces landfill waste.

Practical Explanation:

The main idea is like the foundation of a building, and the supporting details are the bricks that build upon it. Without the foundation, the bricks would have nothing to support them.

Differentiating Between the Main Idea and Supporting Details

To improve your reading skills, it is crucial to distinguish between the main idea and supporting details. The main idea provides the overall topic of the text, while the supporting details offer extra information to support it.

Example:

Consider the following paragraph:

"Playing video games can be beneficial for young people. They improve hand-eye coordination, enhance problem-solving skills, and promote social interaction in multiplayer games."

- **Main Idea:** Playing video games can be beneficial.
- **Supporting Details:** Improve hand-eye coordination, enhance problem-solving skills, and promote social interaction.

Identifying Main Idea vs. Supporting Details

Passage	Main Idea	Supporting Details
Dogs make great pets because they are loyal, affectionate, and provide companionship.	Dogs make great pets	Loyal, affectionate, provide companionship
Exercise is crucial for maintaining physical and mental health. It helps reduce stress, boosts energy, and improves mood.	Exercise is crucial for health	Reduces stress, boosts energy, improves mood

Strategies to Identify the Main Idea

Key Strategies:

- **Look at the Title**: Titles often hint at the main idea.
- **Pay Attention to the First and Last Sentences**: The main idea is frequently found in these locations.
- **Ask, "What's the Point?"**: After reading, ask yourself what the author wants you to know or believe.
- **Summarize in One Sentence**: Try to distill the paragraph or passage into one concise sentence.

Example Strategy in Action:

If you're reading an article titled "Why Healthy Eating Matters," and the first sentence talks about the benefits of nutrition, the main idea is likely about the importance of eating healthy. Summarizing it in one sentence could be: "Healthy eating is essential for maintaining a balanced life."

Practical Example: Finding the Main Idea in a News Article:

Activity Setup:

- Students are provided with a short news article, such as one on climate change or a recent tech innovation, and are asked to find the main idea.

Example:

- *"A new study reveals that electric cars could reduce air pollution by up to 30% in major cities. The research emphasizes the importance of transitioning to renewable energy sources to combat climate change."*

- Main Idea: Electric cars can significantly reduce air pollution and contribute to fighting climate change.

Applying the Strategy

Title	First Sentence	Main Idea
Electric Cars and Pollution Reduction	A new study reveals that electric cars could reduce air pollution by up to 30% in major cities.	Electric cars can reduce air pollution.

Read a Short Passage and Identify the Main Idea

Read the passage below and identify the main idea.

"Social media has changed the way we communicate. It allows people to connect across the world instantly, share ideas, and express opinions. However, it also presents challenges, such as misinformation and privacy concerns."

- ***Main Idea***: Social media has transformed communication, offering both opportunities and challenges.

Trivia Corner

- **Ancient Egypt**: Hieroglyphics were a complex writing system that required advanced reading comprehension skills.

- **Greek Mythology**: Homer's epic poems, The Iliad and The Odyssey, were foundational Western literature texts requiring significant reading comprehension.

- **Renaissance Humanism**: The Renaissance saw a renewed interest in classical texts, which led to advancements in reading comprehension and literacy.

- **The Printing Press**: The invention of the printing press in the 15th century made books more accessible, leading to increased literacy and reading comprehension.

- **The Enlightenment:** The Enlightenment era emphasized reason and knowledge, leading to a focus on reading comprehension and education.

- **The Industrial Revolution:** The Industrial Revolution led to a demand for literate workers, driving the development of public education systems and improving reading comprehension skills.

- **World War II**: Propaganda played a significant role in the war, and the ability to understand and critically evaluate information was crucial.

- **The Civil Rights Movement**: Reading comprehension was essential for understanding and analyzing legal documents, speeches, and other materials related to the Civil Rights Movement.

- **The Digital Age:** The rise of the internet and digital media has changed how we consume information, but reading comprehension remains essential for understanding and evaluating online content.

- **Global Literacy**: Despite technological advancements, illiteracy remains a significant problem in many parts of the world, highlighting the importance of reading comprehension for societal development.

ACTIVITY CORNER 2

1) Activity Exercise: Main Idea Matching

Match the main ideas with the appropriate supporting details.

- **Main Ideas:**
    a. Main Idea A: Recycling helps reduce waste in landfills.
    b. Main Idea B: Regular sleep improves memory and focus.
    c. Main Idea C: Eating fruits and vegetables promotes a healthy lifestyle.

- **Supporting Details:**
    - Detail 1: Sleep helps consolidate memories and improve cognitive function.
    - Detail 2: Recycling paper and plastic reduces the amount of waste in landfills.
    - Detail 3: Fruits and vegetables provide essential vitamins and nutrients.

2) Main Idea Identification Quiz

Provide a series of short passages, and ask students to identify the main idea.

Passage 1:
"The internet has revolutionized the way we communicate. From social media to instant messaging, we can connect with people worldwide within seconds."

- **Question: What is the main idea of this passage?**

Passage 2:
"Exercising regularly helps improve your physical health by strengthening muscles, improving cardiovascular function, and enhancing flexibility."

- **Question: What is the main idea of this passage?**

3) Find the Main Idea in a News Article

Give students a short excerpt from a news article and ask them to find the main idea.
Article Excerpt:

"A recent study conducted by environmental scientists shows that urban green spaces are essential for reducing city air pollution. The researchers found that areas with more trees and parks had lower levels of harmful pollutants in the air. This is a key finding for city planners looking to improve air quality."

- **Question: What is the main idea of this news article?**

3. Recognizing Supporting Details

What are the Supporting Details?

Definition: Supporting details, such as facts, statistics, examples, anecdotes, or explanations, reinforce the main idea.

Example:

Main Idea: Exercise is essential for maintaining a healthy lifestyle.

Supporting Details:

- *Regular exercise reduces the risk of chronic diseases like heart disease and diabetes.*
- *Studies show that people who exercise regularly have lower stress levels.*
- *Exercise improves mental health by releasing endorphins, which boost mood.*

How to Locate Supporting Information in a Text

Strategies:

- Look for Keywords: Words like "because," "for example," "such as," and "according to" often signal that supporting details are being introduced.
- Focus on Evidence: Supporting details are often factual information, examples, or reasoning provided to explain or justify the main idea.
- Ask Questions: Ask, "What is proving or explaining the main idea in this passage?" This will help you pinpoint supporting details.

Main Idea	Supporting Details
Healthy eating prevents disease	1. Fruits and vegetables are high in vitamins and nutrients. 2. A diet rich in antioxidants can help prevent cancer. 3. Whole grains promote heart health.

Importance of Supporting Details in Strengthening Arguments

Explanation: Supporting details provide credibility to an argument, making abstract ideas concrete and convincing readers of the claim's validity.

Example:

Claim: Recycling helps reduce environmental pollution.

Supporting Details:
- Recycling reduces the need for raw materials, which lowers emissions from production.
- According to an EPA study, recycling aluminum saves 95% of the energy required to produce new aluminum.
- Recycled paper requires less water and fewer chemicals to process than new paper.

Practical Example: Analyzing a Persuasive Essay for Supporting Details

Passage:

"School uniforms should be mandatory in all schools. Uniforms help reduce distractions in the classroom and create a sense of unity among students. According to a National Center for Education Statistics study, schools with uniforms report fewer instances of bullying and violence. Additionally, uniforms alleviate pressure on students to wear expensive clothes, which can create social divisions."

Activity: Identify the supporting details in the passage that reinforce the claim that school uniforms should be mandatory.

Answer:

Supporting Details

- Uniforms help reduce distractions in the classroom.
- Uniforms create a sense of unity among students.

- Schools with uniforms report fewer instances of bullying and violence.
- Uniforms alleviate pressure on students to wear expensive clothes, reducing social divisions.

Exercise: Highlight Supporting Details in a Given Passage

Instructions:

Read the following passage and highlight the supporting details supporting the main idea.

Passage:

"Sleep is vital for maintaining overall health. According to the CDC, adults who get at least 7 hours of sleep per night are less likely to develop chronic diseases such as heart disease and diabetes. Studies also show that sufficient sleep improves cognitive function, helping individuals stay alert and focused during the day."

Answer:
- Supporting Details:
    a. Adults with at least 7 hours of sleep are less likely to develop chronic diseases.
    b. Sufficient sleep improves cognitive function.
    c. Sleep helps individuals stay alert and focused during the day.

Supporting Details Often Double as Evidence to Convince the Reader

- *Explanation:* Supporting details often take the form of factual evidence. This evidence strengthens the argument and makes it more persuasive to the reader.
- *Example:*
- Claim: Climate change is accelerating due to human activities.
- Supporting Evidence:

    a. According to NASA, global temperatures have increased by 1.2°C since the late 19th century.
    b. Ice sheets in Greenland and Antarctica have been losing mass alarmingly over the past two decades.
    c. The Intergovernmental Panel on Climate Change (IPCC) reports that human-caused carbon emissions are the primary driver of global warming.

TRIVIA CORNER

10 Little-Known Facts about Famous Books and Their Supporting Arguments

- **"To Kill a Mockingbird" by Harper Lee:** The novel uses real historical cases like the Scottsboro Boys trial as supporting details to address racism and injustice.

- **"1984" by George Orwell:** Orwell's warnings about government surveillance were based on actual totalitarian regimes in history, such as Nazi Germany and Stalinist Russia.

- **"Frankenstein" by Mary Shelley:** Shelley supported her arguments about the dangers of unchecked scientific experimentation with real contemporary scientific breakthroughs, like Galvanism.

- **"Moby Dick" by Herman Melville:** Melville drew on real-life whaling experiences and news accounts of shipwrecks and whale attacks as supporting details to lend authenticity to his narrative.

- **"The Great Gatsby" by F. Scott Fitzgerald:** Fitzgerald used the socio-economic realities of the 1920s, like the rise of the nouveau riche, to support his critique of the American Dream.

- **"The Catcher in the Rye" by J.D. Salinger:** The novel uses real psychological struggles, reflective of Salinger's own experiences, to support its portrayal of teenage angst.

- **"Fahrenheit 451" by Ray Bradbury:** Bradbury used historical instances of censorship, including book burnings by Nazis, as supporting details for his dystopian vision of a society where books are banned.

- **"Brave New World" by Aldous:** Huxley drew on real genetic engineering and consumerism developments to support his satirical portrayal of a future society obsessed with control and pleasure.

- **"The Diary of Anne Frank":** Anne Frank's real-life experiences provide the supporting details for her reflections on war, hope, and humanity.

- **"Pride and Prejudice" by Jane Austen:** Austen's observations of social customs, marriage, and class in early 19th-century England supported her commentary on social expectations.

🎯 ACTIVITY CORNER 3

Exercise 1: True or False - Supporting Details

- **Instructions:** Read the statements below and identify whether they support the main idea correctly. Mark the statements as True or False.
- **Main Idea**: Regular exercise improves physical health.

1. Exercise helps strengthen the heart, reducing the risk of heart disease.
2. Watching TV for long periods helps lower stress.
3. Exercise boosts metabolism, aiding in weight management.
4. Regular exercise can improve mood by releasing endorphins.
5. Eating junk food every day contributes to a healthy lifestyle.

Activity 2: Main Idea and Supporting Details Match

Instructions: Match the main ideas with their correct supporting details.

Main Ideas:

a. Main Idea A: Climate change significantly impacts global weather patterns.
b. Main Idea B: Eating a balanced diet is essential for maintaining a healthy lifestyle.
c. Main Idea C: Technology has improved the way people communicate.

Supporting Details:

- Detail 1: Online communication tools like email and social media allow people to connect instantly across long distances.
- Detail 2: Rising global temperatures are causing more frequent and intense storms and wildfires.
- Detail 3: Consuming fruits, vegetables, and whole grains helps provide essential nutrients and maintain body function.

ACTIVITY CORNER 3

Exercise 3: Passage Annotation

Instructions: Read the passage below and annotate (underline or highlight) the supporting details supporting the main idea.

Passage:
"Renewable energy sources, such as wind and solar power, are becoming increasingly important for addressing climate change. Solar energy reduces reliance on fossil fuels, a major carbon emission source. Wind power provides a clean, renewable alternative to coal and natural gas and can be generated on a large scale without contributing to air pollution."

Question: What are the supporting details?

Activity 4: Fill in the Gaps

Instructions: Fill in the blanks with the appropriate supporting details that reinforce the main idea.

Main Idea: Education is the key to reducing poverty.

a. _____ helps individuals gain the skills needed to find better-paying jobs.
b. Studies have shown that _____ leads to improved economic outcomes for entire communities.
c. Access to _____ increases opportunities for social mobility and personal growth.

4. Inference and Interpretation Skills

What is an Inference?

Definition:

Inference involves drawing conclusions based on evidence and reasoning rather than direct statements in the text. It entails interpreting context clues and understanding the author's implicit meaning.

Example:

Imagine reading a sentence like this: "Sarah looked out the window and saw dark clouds forming on the horizon. She quickly grabbed an umbrella before leaving the house."

Although the text doesn't directly say it will rain here, you can infer from the dark clouds and her grabbing an umbrella that Sarah expects it to rain soon.

Direct Statements vs. Inferences

Direct Statement	Inference
The ground was wet.	It probably rained earlier.
John was trembling and pale.	John is either scared or very cold.
The classroom was silent when the bell rang.	The students may have been focused, or the teacher was absent.

How to Make Logical Inferences from the Text

Steps to Making Inferences:

- Steps to Making Inferences

- Connect the dots between what is written and what is implied.
- Use prior knowledge to make educated guesses.
- Check your inference to ensure it aligns with the overall text and context.

Example:

Passage: "The leaves crunched beneath her feet, and she tightened her scarf against the chill in the air."

Inference: It is probably autumn or winter because the leaves are crunchy, indicating they are dry and fallen, and the character is wearing a scarf due to the cold.

Key Interpretation Strategies for Complex Texts

When encountering complex texts, such as dense literary works, technical writing, or abstract poetry, these strategies can help you interpret the meaning more effectively:

- **Break Down the Text**: Divide the text into smaller, manageable sections and focus on one part at a time.
- **Look for Patterns**: Identify recurring themes, motifs, or symbols that suggest the author's intended message.
- **Pay Attention to Tone and Mood**: Tone can give insight into the author's attitude toward the subject, while mood reflects the atmosphere of the text.
- **Contextualize**: Consider the historical or cultural context in which the text was written, which might influence its meaning.
- **Use Annotation:** Highlight key phrases, make notes in the margins, and ask questions as you read to keep track of your interpretations.

Example:
Excerpt from Shakespeare's Macbeth: "Out, out, brief candle! Life's but a walking shadow, a poor player that struts and frets his hour upon the stage."
Interpretation: Macbeth reflects on the futility of life, comparing it to a fleeting shadow or a bad actor, conveying his deep despair and hopelessness.

Practical Example: Making Inferences from a Mystery Story

Story Excerpt:
"Detective Wilson stepped into the abandoned house. The furniture was covered in dust, and the smell of decay lingered in the air. A broken picture frame lay next to the shattered glass on the floor. He knelt and examined a footprint in the dust by the doorway."

Inference Exercise:

What can you infer about the situation based on this information?
- The house has likely been abandoned for some time due to the dust and decay.
- The broken picture frame and shattered glass may suggest a struggle or incident occurred.
- The footprint near the door indicates someone has recently entered or left the house despite its abandoned state.

Exercise: Infer the Meaning of a Paragraph Based on Contextual Clues

Paragraph:
"Tom hesitated at the platform's edge, staring at the tracks below. His hands were clenched into fists, and his breath came in short, shallow bursts. He heard the train rumbling approaching but couldn't bring himself to move. A crowd pushed past him, oblivious to his inner turmoil."

Question: What can you infer about Tom's emotional state and why he hesitated?

Inference:
Tom is likely feeling overwhelmed, anxious, or even fearful. His clenched fists and shallow breathing suggest that he may be experiencing a panic attack or severe nervousness. His hesitation implies that he is conflicted about whether to board the train or perhaps even facing a deeper emotional decision.

Trivia Corner

- Sherlock Holmes was not the first fictional detective—Edgar Allan Poe's character, C. Auguste Dupin, predated Sherlock Holmes as the world's first fictional detective and also used inference skills to solve crimes.

- Agatha Christie's novels often rely on the reader's ability to make inferences. In her mystery novels, crucial details are left implied, requiring readers to infer the truth behind the crime.

- The Harry Potter series is filled with subtle inferences. For instance, in The Half-Blood Prince, Snape's character development hinges on inferences about his intentions, which are only fully revealed in the final book.

- Hemingway's "Iceberg Theory" encourages readers to infer hidden meaning beneath the surface of the text. He believed that the deeper meaning of a story should not be explicitly stated but inferred by the reader.

- In To Kill a Mockingbird, the character of Boo Radley is misunderstood based on town gossip and fear. Only by making inferences from his actions do the characters and readers come to see his true, protective nature.

- Jane Austen's novels often rely on inference, especially in Pride and Prejudice. Much of the romantic tension is derived from the characters' misunderstandings and unspoken feelings, requiring readers to infer their true emotions.

- The word "inference" comes from the Latin inferred, meaning "to bring in." This reflects the process of incorporating external knowledge or assumptions into the reading of a text.

- The shortest novel is often attributed to Ernest Hemingway's six-word story: "For sale: baby shoes, never worn." This relies entirely on inference for its emotional impact.

- Fairy tales often demand inference – In stories like Little Red Riding Hood, the reader must infer that the wolf's behavior is suspicious before the text explicitly reveals his plan.

- Politicians often imply certain viewpoints or actions in political speeches, leaving it to the audience to infer their intended meaning, a technique known as "dog whistle politics."

ACTIVITY CORNER 4
Activity: Inference and Interpretation Skills

Activity 1: Inferring Character Motives :

Objective: Practice making inferences about character motives based on dialogue and actions.

Instructions: Read the following passage and answer the questions by inferring the motives behind the characters' actions.

Passage:

"As the sun set, Maria anxiously glanced at the clock. Her phone buzzed, but she didn't pick it up. Instead, she quickly grabbed her coat and headed for the door, glancing over her shoulder before she stepped outside."

Questions:
1. Why didn't Maria answer her phone?
2. What can you infer about her feelings as she left the house?
3. Why might Maria have looked over her shoulder before leaving?
4. What could be the reason for her anxiousness when looking at the clock?
5. What inference can you make about Maria's relationship with the person calling her?

Activity 2 Inferring from Dialogue :

Objective: Practice drawing inferences from a conversation between two characters.

Instructions: Read the dialogue and infer details about the characters' relationship, emotions, and the situation.

Dialogue:

Sarah: "I can't believe you did that, Mark. You promised!"
Mark: "I know, Sarah, but it wasn't that simple. I had no choice."
Sarah: "No choice? You always have a choice."
Mark: "Not this time."

Questions:
1. What can you infer about Sarah's feelings toward Mark's actions?
2. What might Mark have done to upset Sarah?

ACTIVITY CORNER 4
Activity: Inference and Interpretation Skills

3. How does Mark feel about his actions based on his response?
4. What inference can you make about their relationship?
5. Based on Mark's statement, "Not this time," what can you infer about the situation?

Activity 3: Inferences from Context Clues

Objective: Infer the meaning of unfamiliar words or phrases from context clues within a passage.

Instructions: Read the passage and infer the meaning of the underlined words based on the context.

Passage:

"The dilapidated house stood on the edge of town, its once-grand facade now crumbling and covered in vines. The townspeople whispered rumors about ghosts and strange occurrences within its walls, but no one dared to enter the house after dark. It was, after all, said to be maleficent, where only bad things happened."

Questions:

1. What does dilapidated likely mean based on the passage?
2. What can you infer about the meaning of the facade from the sentence?
3. How does the word maleficent contribute to the atmosphere of the passage?
4. What inferences can you make about the townspeople's attitude toward the house?
5. What overall tone can you infer from the passage?

5. Analyzing the Author's Purpose and Tone

Understanding Author's Purpose

The author's purpose is why they wrote a particular text. Authors typically write with one of three main purposes in mind:

- **To Persuade:** Convince the reader of a certain point of view or action (e.g., speeches, advertisements, editorials).
- **To Inform**: Provide facts and information (e.g., textbooks, news reports, documentaries).
- **To Entertain**: Engage or amuse the reader (e.g., novels, stories, plays).

Examples of Author's Purpose

Text Type	Author's Purpose
Advertisement	Persuade
News Article	Inform
Comedy Script	Entertain
Opinion Piece	Persuade
History Book	Inform

Practical Example:

Read the following excerpt from an editorial: *"The increasing reliance on fossil fuels is damaging our environment and jeopardizing future generations. Governments must act now to invest in renewable energy sources."*

Questions:
1. What is the author's purpose in this excerpt?
2. How can you tell?

Answer:
The author's purpose is to persuade the reader to support renewable energy and environmental protection, as the language is compelling and urges action.

Recognizing Tone :

The tone is the attitude the author takes toward a subject. It can be:

- **Positive:** Optimistic, hopeful, enthusiastic (e.g., "The future is bright.")
- **Negative:** Pessimistic, critical, frustrated (e.g., "The situation is hopeless.")
- **Neutral**: Objective, impartial, balanced (e.g., "The data shows an increase in temperatures.")

Common Tone Words

Tone	Tone Words
Positive	Hopeful, Encouraging, Enthusiastic, Inspiring
Negative	Angry, Critical, Disappointed, Cynical
Neutral	Informative, Objective, Unbiased, Factual

Practical Example:

Read the excerpt from a speech: "We have the power to change the course of history. Our efforts to tackle climate change have never been more important, and together, we will succeed."

Questions:

1. *What is the tone of the speaker?*
2. *How does the tone influence the reader's perception?*

Answer:

The tone is positive and hopeful, which encourages and empowers the audience to take action on climate change.

Practical Example: Identifying Tone in Political Speeches and Articles :

Excerpt 1:

"We are witnessing a dangerous decline in public trust in our institutions. If we do not act now, we may lose our democracy to cynicism and indifference."

Questions:

1. What is the tone of the speaker?
2. How does the tone reflect the speaker's attitude toward the issue?

Answer:

The tone is negative and critical, expressing concern about the decline in trust and the potential consequences for democracy.

Excerpt 2:

"This community has shown remarkable resilience in the face of adversity. From natural disasters to economic challenges, we have come together stronger than ever."

Questions:

1. What is the tone of the speaker?
2. How does the tone influence the audience's perception of the community?

Answer:

The tone is positive and uplifting. It highlights the community's strength and resilience, fostering a sense of pride and unity.

Exercise: Determine the Author's Purpose and Tone in a Passage :

Passage:

"The polar bear population is shrinking at an alarming rate due to the sea ice loss caused by global warming. Scientists urge immediate action to protect these endangered species and their habitats."

Questions:

1. What is the author's purpose?
2. What tone does the author use?
3. How does the tone help convey the author's message?
4. Why is it important to recognize the tone when reading informational texts?

Answer Key:

1. To let the reader know about the dangers polar bears face due to global warming.
2. The tone is concerned and urgent.
3. The concerned tone emphasizes the seriousness of the situation and the need for action.
4. Recognizing tone helps readers understand the author's attitude and strengthens the information's impact.

Trivia: How an Author's Background Influences Their Tone

- Did you know? An author's personal experiences, cultural background, and political views often influence the tone of their writing. For example, writers from marginalized communities may use a tone of resilience or advocacy.

- Fun Fact: J.K. Rowling's experience as a single mother in financial hardship influenced the tone of perseverance and hope throughout the Harry Potter series.

10 examples of purpose and tone:

Text Type	Purpose	Tone
Editorial on Climate Change	Persuade	Urgent, Concerned
Documentary on Wildlife Conservation	Inform	Neutral, Factual
Satirical Article on Politics	Entertain	Humorous, Sarcastic
Motivational Speech for Graduates	Inspire	Uplifting, Encouraging
Travel Blog Post on a Beach Resort	Entertain, Inform	Relaxed, Enthusiastic
Scientific Journal on Medicine	Inform	Objective, Analytical
Political Campaign Speech	Persuade	Passionate, Assertive
Poem about Nature	Entertain, Evoke Emotion	Reflective, Appreciative
Advertisement for a Charity	Persuade	Compassionate, Urgent
Autobiography of a Survivor	Inform, Inspire	Somber, Hopeful
Movie Review Blog	Entertain, Inform	Critical, Witty
Historical Fiction Novel	Entertain	Nostalgic, Reflective
News Report on Economic Trends	Inform	Neutral, Factual
Opinion Piece on Education Reform	Persuade	Passionate, Concerned
Humorous Short Story	Entertain	Playful, Lighthearted
Social Media Post on Fitness Motivation	Inspire, Entertain	Encouraging, Energizing
Technical Manual for Software	Inform	Objective, Clear
Personal Blog on Overcoming Challenges	Inform, Inspire	Honest, Hopeful
Children's Storybook	Entertain, Educate	Playful, Imaginative
Letter to the Editor on Social Justice	Persuade	Angry, Urgent

Trivia Corner

- *The Birth of Tone:* The concept of "tone" in literary analysis emerged in the late 19th century, popularized by scholars like Henry James.
- *Purpose and Genre:* An author's purpose often aligns with the genre. For instance, persuasive essays aim to convince, while narrative works often entertain or inform.
- *Twain's Words of Wisdom:* Mark Twain emphasized the power of precise language, stating, "The difference between the almost right word and the right word is a large matter—'tis the difference between the lightning bug and the lightning."
- *Tone's Impact on Perception:* Research suggests tone significantly influences readers' understanding. Subtle shifts can alter a message's meaning, as demonstrated in works like Edgar Allan Poe's "The Tell-Tale Heart."
- *Pride and Prejudice: A Title That Tells:* Jane Austen's original title for "Pride and Prejudice," "First Impressions," accurately reflects her exploration of initial judgments and societal expectations.
- *Shakespeare's Shifting Tones:* Shakespeare masterfully employed tone shifts to signal changes in mood. In "Macbeth," the tone transitions from ambition and suspense to despair and tragedy.
- *Tone and Platform:* Advertisers tailor their tone to different platforms. Social media often calls for a more informal, conversational style, while TV commercials may adopt a more authoritative or persuasive approach.
- *Audience-Centric Tone:* Authors often adjust their tone to resonate with their target audience. Young adult novels typically use more relatable language, while academic papers demand a formal, objective style.
- *Orwell's Dystopian Tone:* George Orwell's "1984" employs a tone of despair, paranoia, and hopelessness to amplify themes of surveillance and control.
- *Neutrality in Non-Fiction:* While non-fiction writers strive for neutrality, subtle language choices can reveal biases or underlying attitudes. For instance, certain adjectives or adverbs can subtly shape a reader's perception.
-

🎯 ACTIVITY CORNER 5

Activity 1: Author's Purpose Quiz (Multiple Choice)

Instructions: Identify the author's purpose for each passage.

1) Passage: "Donate now to help save the environment! Every dollar counts toward preserving our planet."
- A. Entertain
- B. Persuade
- C. Inform
- D. Inspire

2) Passage: "Here are the top 10 reasons why recycling is essential to reducing waste and saving resources."
- A. Inform
- B. Persuade
- C. Entertain
- D. Inspire

3) Passage: "Once upon a time, in a land far, far away, there lived a wise old king who ruled with kindness."
- A. Persuade
- B. Inform
- C. Entertain
- D. Inspire

4) Passage: "You can overcome any obstacle if you believe in yourself and never give up."
- A. Inform
- B. Entertain
- C. Inspire
- D. Persuade

5) Passage: "The annual rainfall in the Amazon rainforest can reach over 120 inches, making it one of the wettest places on Earth."
- A. Inform
- B. Persuade
- C. Entertain
- D. Inspire

Activity 2: Match the Tone with the Passage

Instructions: Match the passage with the correct tone.

Passage	Tone
"The day was filled with laughter and light, a perfect celebration."	Joyful
"He stormed out of the room, slamming the door behind him."	Angry
"The guide carefully explained each step in the process, ensuring clarity."	Calm
"Despite the gloomy weather, there was a certain peace that hung in the air."	Reflective
"She rolled her eyes and sarcastically remarked, 'Oh great, another meeting!'"	Sarcastic

Activity 3: Multiple Choice (Identify the Tone)

Instructions: Choose the tone that best matches the passage.

1) **Passage**: "The politician's speech was filled with anger and accusations, blaming the opposition for all the country's problems."

- A. Optimistic
- B. Angry
- C. Playful
- D. Neutral

2) **Passage:** "The author takes you on a thrilling ride through the city, weaving in and out of traffic in a high-speed chase."

- A. Relaxed
- B. Thrilling
- C. Critical
- D. Informative

3) Passage: "It was hard to tell whether the decision would result in success or failure, as the situation seemed to balance on a knife's edge."

- A. Anxious
- B. Hopeful
- C. Sarcastic
- D. Joyful

4) Passage: "The flowers bloomed with a radiance that filled the garden with joy and peace."

- A. Angry
- B. Reflective
- C. Joyful
- D. Anxious

5) Passage: "The instructor calmly explained the intricate details of the scientific experiment."

- A. Neutral
- B. Excited
- C. Angry
- D. Humorous

ACTIVITY 4: MATCH THE FOLLOWING (AUTHOR'S PURPOSE)

Instructions: Match the passage with the author's purpose: Persuade, Inform, Entertain, or Inspire.

Passage	Author's Purpose
We must act now to combat climate change, before it's too late.	Persuade
The Pacific Ocean is the largest ocean on Earth, covering more than 60 million square miles.	Inform
The man slipped on the banana peel and landed in a puddle, much to the amusement of the crowd.	Entertain
Keep pushing forward, no matter how hard the road ahead may seem.	Inspire

6. Vocabulary in Context

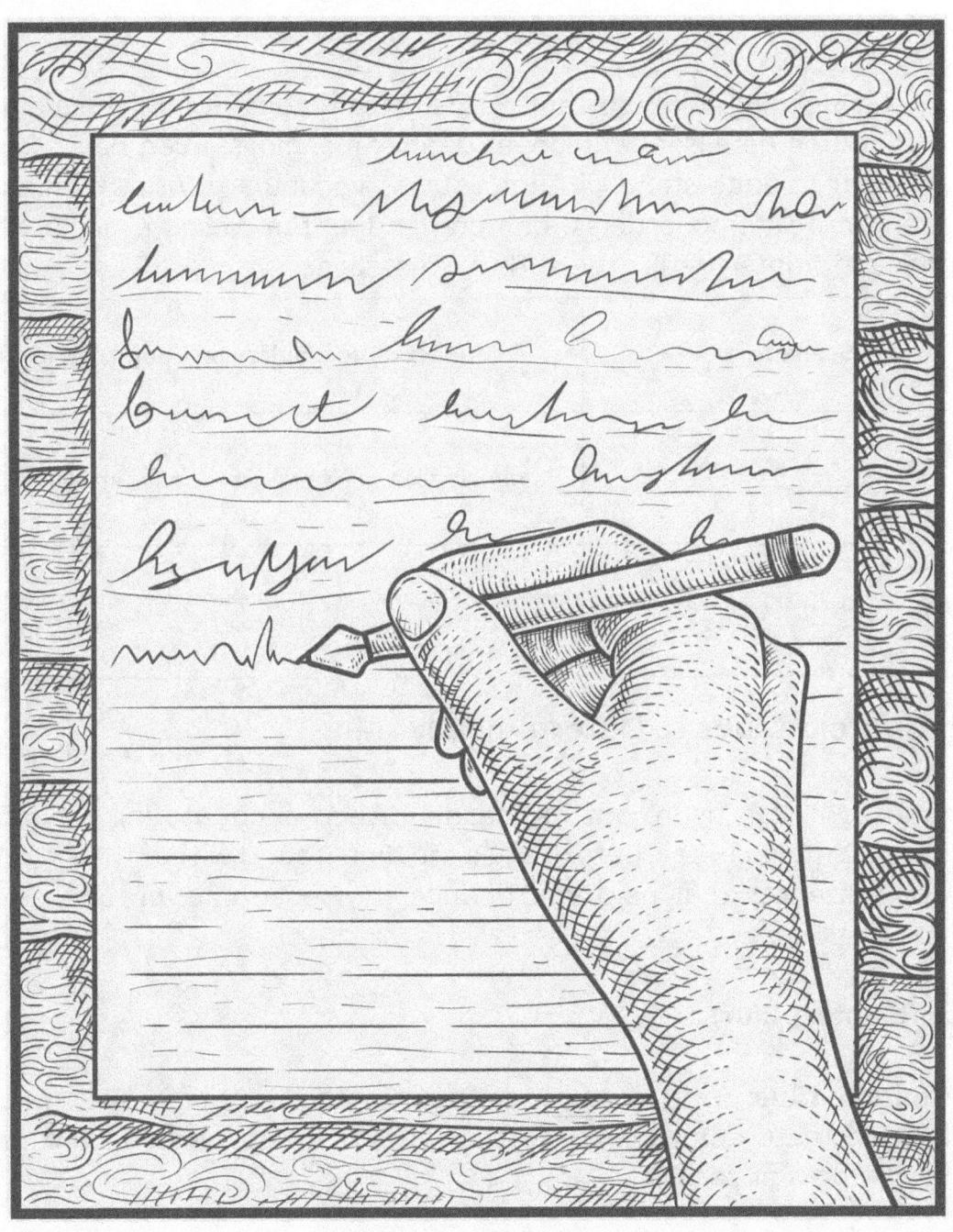

Why Vocabulary Matters in Reading Comprehension :

Understanding vocabulary is crucial for effective communication. It enables us to comprehend the message of a text, convey thoughts clearly, and tackle complex subjects.

Knowing the meanings of important words helps readers follow the main ideas, grasp supporting details, and uncover deeper meanings. Even basic texts can be challenging to understand without a strong vocabulary. Whether it's fiction, nonfiction, or academic articles, comprehending the words used in a text is fundamental for interpreting the author's message.

Scenario	Impact of Vocabulary on Comprehension
You don't understand key words in a passage	You miss the author's main point or misinterpret the details
You understand the vocabulary well	You follow the argument, get the nuances, and comprehend deeply

Using Context Clues to Determine Meaning :

Sometimes, you can figure out its meaning when encountering an unfamiliar word using context clues. Context clues are hints found within the surrounding words or sentences that help you deduce the sense of a problematic word without a dictionary.

Types of Context Clues:

- **Definition Clue:** The word is defined in the sentence. **Example**: "The arboreal creature, meaning one that lives in trees, was spotted swinging through the branches."

- **Synonym Clue:** A similar word is used. **Example:** "The dessert was delectable or extremely delicious."
- **Antonym Clue:** A contrasting word gives you a hint. **Example:** "The class was chaotic, unlike the calm atmosphere of the library."
- **Example Clue:** Examples help illustrate the word's meaning. **Example:** "Her eclectic taste in music includes jazz, pop, and classical."

Practical Example:

Let's take a passage from popular fiction:

"As Harry Potter approached the door, he noticed the ominous clouds gathering overhead. He hesitated, sensing that something dark and dangerous lurked behind the door."

Using context clues (clouds gathering overhead, something dark and dangerous), you can infer that the word ominous likely means something that gives the impression that something terrible or threatening is about to happen.

Exercise: Context Clue Practice

For each sentence below, determine the meaning of the bolded word based on the context clues.

1) The gregarious child made friends with everyone at the party, constantly talking and laughing.- **Meaning**: Social, outgoing

2) Despite his skepticism, he agreed to try the new method just to prove it wouldn't work.- **Meaning**: Doubtful, suspicious

3) The reclusive author rarely gave interviews, choosing to live a quiet life away from the public eye instead.- **Meaning**: Isolated, withdrawn

4) The simple recipe required only essential ingredients like flour, eggs, and sugar—rudimentary.- **Meanin**g: Basic, simple

5) After the thunderstorm, the air felt muggy, hot, and damp, making everyone uncomfortable.- **Meaning**: Humid, sticky

Readers Exposed to a Rich Vocabulary Are 60% More Likely to Comprehend Complex Texts.

According to research, students who regularly encounter new words are far better equipped to understand complex readings, especially in science, history, and literature. Expanding your vocabulary makes you a more confident reader, allowing you to better navigate challenging material, score higher on tests, and enjoy reading more.

Vocabulary Exposure	Comprehension Level
Low exposure to new vocabulary	Struggles with complex texts
High exposure to new vocabulary	Mastery of complex texts

Fascinating Origins of Everyday Words

- Robot: This word comes from the Czech word "robota," which means forced labor or drudgery. It first appeared in Karel Čapek's play R.U.R. (Rossum's Universal Robots) in 1920.

- Malaria: Derived from the Italian words "mal" (bad) and "aria" (air), malaria was once thought to be caused by bad air, especially in swamps and marshlands.

- Quarantine: Originating from the Italian "quaranta giorni," meaning "40 days," it refers to isolating ships suspected of carrying plague for 40 days.

- Salary: The word comes from the Latin word "solarium, " which means payment in salt. Roman soldiers were sometimes paid in salt because it was a valuable commodity.

- Tsunami: This Japanese word translates to "harbor wave" and refers to the large, destructive waves caused by undersea earthquakes.

Trivia Corner

- *The Birth of "Quiz":* While the exact origin of "quiz" is debated, it's widely believed to have been popularized in the late 18th century. Some sources suggest it might be related to a game played in Ireland.

- *The Longest Word:* The longest word in the English dictionary, "pneumonoultramicroscopicsilicovolcanoconiosis," is a medical term referring to a lung disease caused by inhaling silica dust from volcanic ash.

- *"Goodbye" and "God Be With Ye":* The phrase "goodbye" is indeed a contraction of "God be with ye." However, it's important to note that this contraction was common in Middle English and has been used for centuries.

- *The Power of Etymology:* Etymology, the study of word origins, can be a valuable tool for understanding vocabulary. Knowing word roots can help you decipher unfamiliar words and expand your vocabulary.

- *The Origin of "OK":* While the exact origin of "OK" is still debated, one popular theory suggests it might be a misspelling of "all correct" or an abbreviation of "okey-dokey."

- *Emoji: A New Form of Language:* Emojis have become integral to digital communication, offering a visual way to express emotions and ideas. The word "emoji" comes from the Japanese words "e" (picture) and "moji" (character).

- *"Salary" and Salt:* The word "salary" indeed originates from the Latin word "salarium," which referred to a form of payment in ancient Rome. However, salt was not the only form of payment; it was simply one valuable commodity.

- *The "Nerd" Controversy:* While Dr. Seuss is often credited with popularizing the word "nerd," there's evidence that it was used in informal speech before his book "If I Ran the Zoo."

- *"Villain" from Farmworker to Evil-Doer:* The word "villain" originally referred to a farmworker or serf in Old French. Over time, its meaning shifted to describe a person with evil intentions in stories.

- *"Sarcasm" and "Dog-like Tearing":* The word "sarcasm" derives from the Greek word "sarkazein," which means "to tear flesh like dogs." This imagery highlights the biting and hurtful nature of sarcastic remarks.

ACTIVITY CORNER 6

Activity 1: Match the Word with its Definition

Match the vocabulary word with the correct definition.

Word	Definition
1. Ubiquitous	A. Extremely outdated
2. Ephemeral	B. Friendly, warm
3. Antiquated	C. Present everywhere
4. Cordial	D. Short-lived
5. Scrupulous	E. Very careful and attentive to detail

Activity 2: True or False – Vocabulary in Context

Instructions: Read the sentence and determine if the statement about the word is True or False.

1) Sentence: "The scientist's innovative solution revolutionized the industry."
- **Statement:** "Innovative" means traditional.

2) Sentence: "The detective was meticulous in examining the crime scene, ensuring no detail was overlooked."
- **Statement:** "Meticulous" means careless and sloppy.

3) Sentence: "Her benevolent nature led her to volunteer at several charities."
- **Statement**: "Benevolent" means kind and generous.

4) Sentence: "The class was apathetic, showing no interest in the lesson."
- **Statement:** "Apathetic" means enthusiastic and engaged.

5) Sentence: "The debate was contentious, with both sides arguing fiercely."
- **Statement**: "Contentious" means peaceful and harmonious.

🎯 ACTIVITY CORNER 6

Activity 3: Multiple Choice – Context Clues

Instructions: Choose the best definition of the bolded word based on the context clues in the sentence.

1) Sentence: "The detective's astute observations helped solve the complex mystery."
- A. Careless
- B. Sharp, insightful
- C. Confused
- D. Irresponsible

2) Sentence: "The solution seemed inconceivable at first, but eventually, the team found a way to make it work."
- A. Unbelievable
- B. Easy to understand
- C. Ordinary
- D. Simple

3) Sentence: "The convoluted explanation left the audience even more confused than before."
- A. Clear
- B. Complicated, twisted
- C. Simple
- D. Short

4) Sentence: "The placid lake was a perfect spot for a quiet afternoon of reflection."
- A. Calm and peaceful
- B. Busy
- C. Dangerous
- D. Loud

5) Sentence: "The impeccable performance left the judges in awe."
- A. Flawed
- B. Perfect, without fault
- C. Boring
- D. Mediocre

7. Identifying Text Structure

Introduction :

Objective: This chapter will assist high school students in identifying various text structures, enhancing their comprehension skills by enabling them to grasp how information is organized within a passage.

Types of Text Structures

Understanding the organization of a text can provide students with insights into the author's intentions and the connections between ideas. Here are the four main types of text structures:

Text Structure	Description	Signal Words/Examples
Cause and Effect	Explains the reasons why something happened (cause) and the resulting consequences (effect).	Because, therefore, due to, as a result, consequently
Compare and Contrast	Shows similarities and differences between two or more ideas, objects, or events.	Similarly, on the other hand, in contrast, likewise
Chronological	Describes events in the order they occurred, often used in historical texts or process descriptions.	First, then, next, finally, before, after
Problem and Solution	Introduces a problem and then outlines possible solutions to address it.	The problem is, in order to, solve, answer, fix

Why Understanding Structure Helps Comprehension :

Recognizing the structure of a text helps readers:

- Identify key points and organize information more effectively.
- Anticipate what will happen next or how ideas are related.
- Retain information more efficiently because they can mentally group similar ideas.

Benefits of Text Structure in Reading

Benefit	Example
Improves comprehension	Knowing a text is organized by cause and effect helps you see how one event leads to another.
Enhances retention of information	Grouping similar ideas helps you remember details longer.
Helps identify the author's purpose	Recognizing a problem/solution structure suggests the author is providing solutions to issues.
Clarifies the relationship between concepts	Comparing and contrasting two ideas helps clarify their differences and similarities.

Practical Example: Identifying the Structure in a Historical Document

Document Excerpt:

"The Great Depression began in 1929 and resulted in severe economic hardships across the globe. Many people lost their jobs, and banks failed. To combat this crisis, the government introduced a series of programs, collectively known as the New Deal, which aimed to provide economic relief, reform the financial system, and stimulate recovery."

Explanation: This passage uses a Cause and Effect structure. The Great Depression (cause) led to economic hardships (effect). The New Deal programs (solution) were introduced to address these issues (problem and solution).

Exercise: Label the Text Structure in a Paragraph

Instructions: Read each passage and identify the text structure. Choose from Cause and Effect, Compare and Contrast, Chronological, or Problem and Solution.

1) *"The introduction of cell phones changed the way we communicate. Before, people had to rely on landlines, but now, mobile devices have made communication more convenient and immediate."*
- Answer: Compare and Contrast

2) *"To reduce pollution, cities are implementing various strategies such as improving public transportation, increasing green spaces, and encouraging recycling."*
- Answer: Problem and Solution

3) *"First, settlers arrived in the New World. Next, they established colonies. Finally, the colonies grew into thriving communities."*
- Answer: Chronological

4) *"Due to climate change, the polar ice caps are melting rapidly, leading to rising sea levels."*
- Answer: Cause and Effect

5) *"The two political parties have different views on healthcare reform. One party advocates for a public option, while the other prefers a private sector approach."*
- Answer: Compare and Contrast

Recognizing Text Structure Enhances Memory Retention

A study showed that students who learned to identify text structures, such as cause-and-effect or chronological sequences, were 40% more likely to remember key information. Structured content helps the brain create mental frameworks that are easier to recall.

Trivia Corner

- *Did you know? The Problem and Solution structure is often used in political speeches and advertisements to persuade audiences by presenting a compelling issue and offering a desirable solution.*

- *Surprising fact: Autobiographies and memoirs frequently employ a Chronological text structure to guide readers through the author's life experiences sequentially.*

- *Fascinating insight: The Cause and Effect structure is a cornerstone of scientific writing, as it helps explain complex phenomena and their resulting consequences.*

- *Historical trivia: The ancient Greeks were pioneers of compare-and-contrast writing and used this structure to analyze and debate various political systems.*

- *Fun fact: Understanding text structures like Compare and Contrast can enhance your comprehension of literature and subjects like math and science, where comparisons between concepts are essential.*

- *Research shows that chronological text structure is a popular choice in history and social studies textbooks, as it helps students follow the sequence of events and understand their significance.*

- *Did you know? Journalists often rely on the Problem and Solution structure when reporting on social or environmental issues, highlighting the problem, and proposing potential solutions.*

- *Fascinating insight: The Cause and Effect structure is widely used in news articles and documentaries to explain how certain events or decisions have led to significant outcomes.*

- *Surprising stat: Studies have shown that readers who can quickly identify text structure are 50% more likely to understand and remember the material they are reading.*

- *Little-known fact: The problem-solution structure is a common feature in self-help books and guides, offering readers practical advice on overcoming challenges and achieving their goals.*

🎯 ACTIVITY CORNER 7

Activity 1: Match the Structure

Instructions: Match the paragraph excerpts to their correct text structure.

Paragraph Excerpt	Text Structure
1. "First, the settlers arrived. Then, they built homes, and finally, they formed a government."	Chronological
2. "The invention of smartphones led to changes in how we communicate and access information."	Cause and Effect
3. "While both cats and dogs make good pets, cats are more independent, whereas dogs are more social."	Compare and Contrast
4. "Plastic waste is a major issue. To address this, we need to recycle more and reduce consumption."	Problem and Solution
5. "Heavy rain caused flooding across the city, resulting in widespread damage to property."	Cause and Effect

Activity 2: True or False

Instructions: Determine if the following statements are true or false.

1. True or False: Chronological structure always involves comparing two different ideas.
2. True or False: Cause and Effect structure is often used to explain scientific concepts.
3. True or False: In a Problem and Solution text, the solution always appears at the end of the passage.
4. True or False: Compare and Contrast explain the sequence of historical events.
5. True or False: Identifying text structure can help improve reading comprehension.

ACTIVITY CORNER 7

Activity 3: Identify the Structure

Instructions: Read the following passage and identify the text structure used.

Passage 1:
"Many students struggle with time management. To help with this issue, schools have implemented time management workshops, created apps for scheduling tasks, and encouraged students to set daily goals."

Passage 2:
"Throughout the 19th century, many technological advances occurred. The first steam engine was invented, then railways expanded, and later, electric power transformed industries."

Passage 3:
"Pollution levels are rising in urban areas because of increased vehicle emissions and industrial activity, leading to poor air quality."

Activity 4: Text Structure Sorting

Instructions: Read the following passages and sort them into the correct text structure categories: chronological, compare-and-contrast, cause-and-effect, or problem-and-solution. Write the number of each passage under the appropriate heading.

Passages:
1. "Global warming is causing rising sea levels, which leads to increased flooding in coastal areas."
2. "While apples and oranges are both fruits, apples are crisp and sweet, while oranges are juicy and tangy."
3. "The printing press was invented in the 15th century. This was followed by widespread literacy and the circulation of books."
4. "The high dropout rate in schools is a serious problem. One solution could be providing better academic support and counseling."
5. "First, the scientist experimented. Next, the data was analyzed, and the results were published.

8. Summarizing and Paraphrasing

The Art of Summarizing

Summarizing involves condensing a larger text into essential points, capturing critical ideas without losing the original meaning.

Example:

Original Text:

"In the late 19th century, the Industrial Revolution transformed Europe and North America. Factories replaced small workshops, and mass production led to new products, changes in labor, and the growth of cities."

Summary:

"The Industrial Revolution in the late 19th century caused major changes, including the rise of factories and urban growth."

Key Elements of Summarizing

Element	Explanation	Example
Condense Information	Reduce the text to its main ideas	Summarizing an entire article into a few sentences
Eliminate Details	Remove minor or irrelevant details	Leave out specific dates or unnecessary anecdotes
Maintain Core Meaning	Keep the essential ideas and meaning intact	Ensure the summary reflects the original intent
Be Brief	Keep the summary short and concise	Avoid lengthy explanations or unnecessary words

Practical Example: Summarizing a Chapter of a Popular Book

Book Chapter: "Harry Potter and the Sorcerer's Stone" (Chapter 1)

The first chapter introduces Harry Potter, a young orphan living with his unpleasant aunt, uncle, and cousin. He is aware of his magical heritage once mysterious letters are addressed to him.

Summary of Chapter 1:

"Harry Potter, an orphan, lives with his unkind relatives and starts receiving strange letters, hinting at something magical about his past."

Paraphrasing: Retelling in Your Own Words

Paraphrasing is rewording a text using your own words while keeping the original meaning. Unlike summarizing, paraphrasing focuses on translating a passage rather than condensing it.

Example:

Original Sentence:
"The Industrial Revolution was a turning point in history, resulting in significant changes to society, industry, and technology."

Paraphrase:
"The Industrial Revolution marked a major historical shift, bringing important changes to industries, societies, and technologies."

Tip	Explanation	Example
Change the Wording	Use different words or phrases with the same meaning	Original: "essential," Paraphrase: "crucial"
Change the Structure	Rearrange the sentence or paragraph	Original: "It was difficult to manage," Paraphrase: "Managing it proved to be hard."
Maintain Meaning	Keep the original idea intact while altering the language	Paraphrase without changing the text's intent
Avoid Copying	Do not simply replace words with synonyms	Rewrite entire phrases to avoid plagiarism

Practical Example: Paraphrasing a Passage

Original Passage:

"Social media has revolutionized the way we communicate. While it connects people from around the globe, it has also raised concerns about privacy and mental health."

Paraphrase:

"Platforms like social media have transformed communication worldwide. However, they have also sparked debates over privacy and mental well-being."

Practical Example: Summarizing a Chapter of a Popular Book

Original Text:

"The Hunger Games" by Suzanne Collins (Chapter 1)

The first chapter introduces us to Katniss Everdeen, a teenager living in the impoverished District 12 of the dystopian nation of Panem. She hunts illegally to provide food for her family, and we learn about the cruel annual event called the Hunger Games, in which children fight to the death for the entertainment of the Capitol.

Summary of Chapter 1:

"Katniss Everdeen, a young girl in a dystopian world, hunts to feed her family and lives in a society where children must participate in the brutal Hunger Games."

Exercise: Summarize a Passage in 3-5 Sentences

Passage:

"Climate change is an urgent issue affecting the entire planet. Rising global temperatures have led to melting ice caps, rising sea levels, and more frequent extreme weather events such as hurricanes and droughts. Efforts to combat climate change include reducing carbon emissions, transitioning to renewable energy, and preserving natural ecosystems."

Summary:

"Climate change is causing melting ice caps, rising sea levels, and extreme weather. To address this, reducing carbon emissions and transitioning to renewable energy are key strategies."

Summarizing Boosts Information Retention

Research shows that summarizing forces the brain to process and reorganize information, leading to better understanding and memory retention. Summarizing enhances comprehension and improves critical thinking and recall in future readings. This skill benefits academic success and real-life applications, such as studying for exams or analyzing complex topics.

Final Thoughts

By mastering both summarizing and paraphrasing, students improve their reading comprehension and become more effective writers and communicators. These skills are crucial in academic settings and in everyday communication, whether analyzing books or articles or understanding complex topics at work or in life.

Trivia Corner

- **Moby Dick:** Often oversimplified as a tale of man vs. beast, Moby Dick is a complex exploration of obsession, revenge, and the nature of evil, with the whale serving as a symbol of the universe's indifference.

- **1984:** More than just a dystopian fantasy, 1984 is a scathing critique of totalitarianism, surveillance, and the erosion of individual freedom in a world controlled by a powerful government.

- **The Great Gatsby:** While it's a love story on the surface, The Great Gatsby is a poignant commentary on the American Dream, class distinctions, and the corrupting influence of wealth and materialism.

- **Pride and Prejudice**: Beyond a romance, Pride and Prejudice is a sharp satire of social norms, gender roles, and the importance of class and marriage in 19th-century England.

- **Frankenstein:** More than a horror story about a monster, Frankenstein is a profound exploration of scientific ethics, human hubris, and the consequences of playing God.

- **The Catcher in the Rye:** While it's often seen as a coming-of-age story, The Catcher in the Rye is a deep exploration of alienation, identity crises, and the loss of innocence in a world that seems increasingly phony.

- **Animal Farm**: More than a children's fable, Animal Farm is a powerful political allegory that satirizes the Russian Revolution and the corrupting influence of power.

- **To Kill a Mockingbird**: While it's a story about racial injustice, It is also a profound exploration of childhood, morality, and the human condition.

- **Lord of the Flies:** More than a simple tale of boys on an island, Lord of the Flies is a deep exploration of human nature, societal collapse, and the destructive forces within us all.

- **The Odyssey:** While it's an adventure story, The Odyssey is also a complex exploration of heroism, fate, and the human condition, with themes of loyalty, family, and the power of storytelling.

 ACTIVITY CORNER 8

Activity 1: Match the Paraphrases

Instructions: Match each original sentence with the correct paraphrase.

Original Sentences	Paraphrases
1. "Global warming is causing glaciers to melt at an alarming rate, leading to rising sea levels."	A. Rising sea levels are the result of glaciers melting rapidly due to global warming.
2. "The invention of the internet has revolutionized the way we communicate and access information."	B. The internet has dramatically changed communication and how we obtain information.
3. "Eating a balanced diet and exercising regularly are key factors in maintaining good health."	C. Regular exercise and a nutritious diet are essential for staying healthy.

Activity 2: True or False – Summarizing

Instructions: Read the following statements about summarizing and mark them as true or false.

1. Summarizing involves restating the text with more detail.
2. A summary should include the main points and supporting details.
3. Summaries should be brief and to the point.
4. Summarizing is the same as paraphrasing.
5. Summarizing helps with better retention of information.

Activity 3: Match the Author's Purpose

Instructions: Match each text description with the author's purpose: Persuade, Inform, or Entertain.

Text Description	Author's Purpose
1. An advertisement urging people to adopt healthy eating habits.	
2. A biography detailing the life of Albert Einstein.	A. Persuade
3. A novel about a group of friends going on a thrilling adventure.	B. Inform
4. A news article explaining the latest developments in climate change research.	C. Entertain
5. A speech encouraging people to donate to a charity organization.	

Activity 4: Identify the Main Idea and Summarize

Instructions: Read the following short passage. Identify the main idea and write a summary in 1-2 sentences.

Passage:

"Artificial Intelligence (AI) is rapidly advancing and transforming industries such as healthcare, finance, and education. AI-powered tools can now diagnose diseases, predict stock market trends, and create personalized learning experiences. However, the rapid growth of AI has also raised ethical concerns about privacy, security, and job displacement."

9. Reading Beyond the Text: Critical Thinking and Reflection

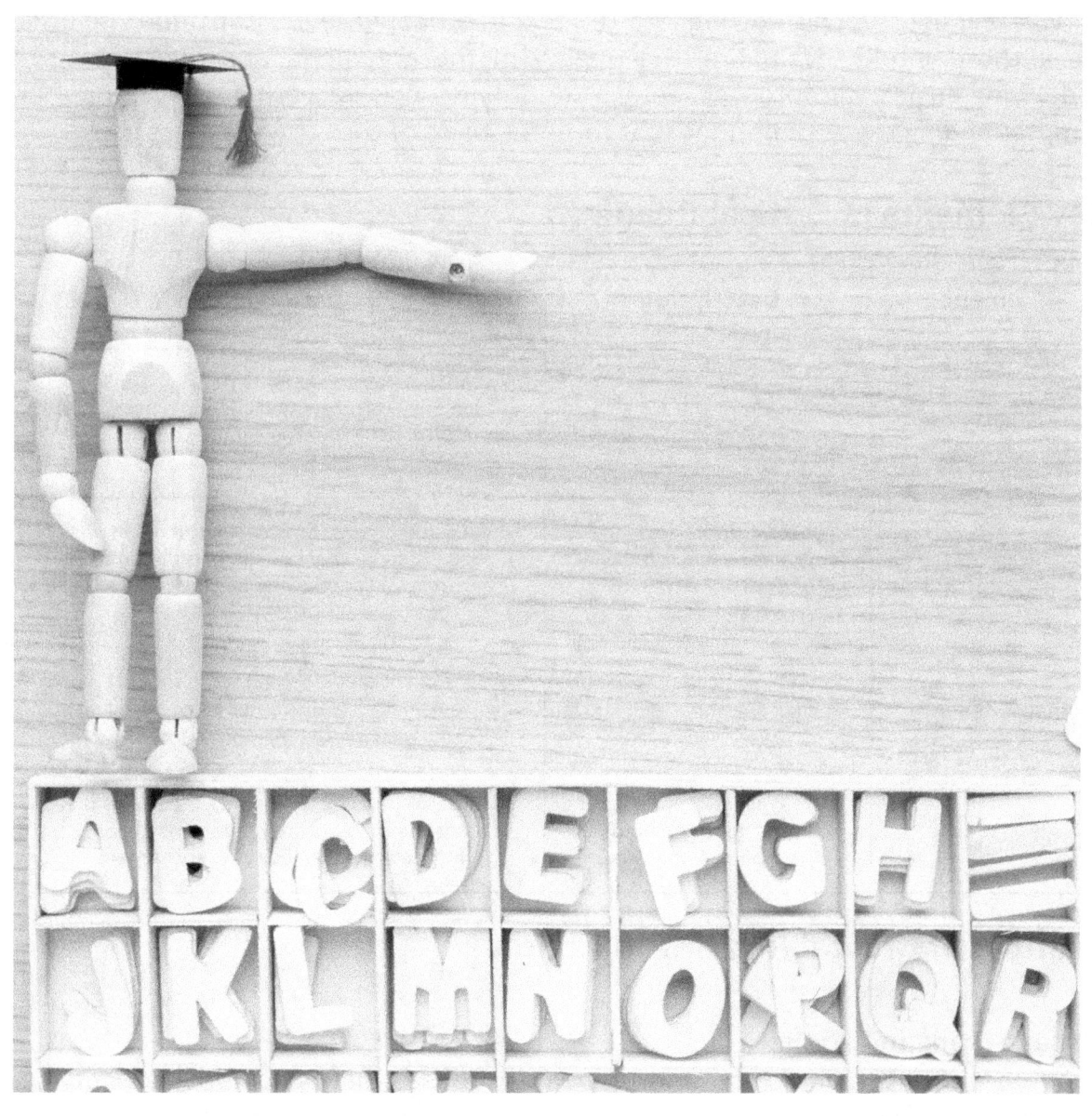

Reading beyond the text involves more than understanding what is written. It requires you to engage critically and reflectively with the material. In this chapter, we will explore how to read with a critical eye, ask deeper questions, and reflect on the text by connecting it to personal experiences. Through practice and reflection, you'll learn how to become a more thoughtful and insightful reader.

Reading with a Critical Eye

Critical reading involves delving into the text at a deeper level. It includes analyzing the author's intent, evaluating the quality of the argument, and questioning the underlying logic. This process entails identifying biases, verifying evidence, and comprehending the assumptions that form the basis of the author's message.

Key Elements of Critical Reading

Element	Description	Example
Identifying Bias	Recognizing the author's preferences or partiality.	A political commentator writing an article about education reform may favor one political party's stance on the issue. You should ask: Is this opinion skewing the facts?
Evaluating Evidence	Checking if the evidence provided is reliable, relevant, and from trustworthy sources.	A writer cites a study showing the benefits of meditation for mental health. Is this study peer-reviewed, and are the results consistent with other research?
Assessing Logic	Determining if the argument is logically structured and free of fallacies.	An argument that says, "All teens should stop using social media because some teens have negative experiences with it" is a hasty generalization.
Understanding Assumptions	Identifying assumptions the author takes for granted but does not explicitly state.	An essay on homework policies assumes that all students have stable internet access at home. Is this assumption valid for every student?

Example of Critical Reading in Action

Passage from an Article
"School uniforms should be mandatory because they promote equality and discipline. A survey showed that 90% of students at a private school believe uniforms are beneficial."

Critical Reading Response :

- **Identifying Bias:** The author seems to promote uniforms without considering opposing viewpoints.

- **Evaluating Evidence:** Is the survey reliable? Were public school students included?

- **Assessing Logic**: Does one survey prove that uniforms promote equality?

- **Understanding Assumptions**: The author assumes that uniforms lead to equality without considering other factors, such as school environment or socio-economic differences.

Asking Deeper Questions

While surface-level questions address basic text elements, critical questions probe underlying meanings and intentions to uncover the author's motives.

Examples of Deeper Questions

Surface-Level Question	Deeper Critical Question
What is the author's main argument?	Why does the author present this argument? What personal, cultural, or historical factors may have influenced this perspective?
What evidence does the author use?	How reliable is this evidence? Is it backed by credible sources, or does it lack sufficient support?
What is the author's tone?	How does the tone shape the reader's perception of the issue? Does the tone influence how convincing or biased the argument seems?

Example: After reading a newspaper editorial about climate change, a surface-level question might be: *"What is the author's main argument?"*
A deeper critical question would be: *"Why does the author focus on the economic costs of climate change mitigation without discussing long-term environmental impacts?"*

Reflecting on the Text: Connecting with Personal Experiences

Reflective reading involves relating the text to personal experiences or broader social issues, deepening understanding, and encouraging emotional and intellectual engagement with the text.

Example: Reflective Reading

"A young character in a novel faces challenges when moving to a new city, struggling to make friends and adjust to a different school environment."

Reflection:

"This reminds me of when I moved to a new school in eighth grade. I had similar struggles making friends at first, but I found ways to connect with people over time. Reading about this character's experiences made me think about how I overcame my difficulties and how important it is to be resilient in new situations."

Reflecting on personal experiences can help one understand a text deeper, often drawing connections that enhance comprehension and empathy.

Reflection Connections

Text Example	Personal Reflection
A historical text about civil rights activism.	Reading this makes me think about modern-day protests and movements. I wonder how past actions have influenced current activism.
A story about someone facing failure before succeeding.	I can relate this to my own experience in sports, where I failed at first but eventually improved by working harder.

Practical Example: Critically Analyzing a Newspaper Editorial

To practice critical reading and reflection, let's analyze the following editorial passage about climate change:

Editorial Passage:

"Climate change has taken center stage in global discussions in recent years. However, some argue that the severity of climate change is exaggerated. Critics claim that the measures being taken, such as reducing emissions and investing in green energy, are costly and inefficient. Meanwhile, supporters of environmental policies argue that ignoring climate change will have catastrophic consequences."

Critical Analysis Questions:

1) What evidence does the author present for both sides?
The editorial presents critics' concerns about the cost and efficiency of climate measures and supporters' warnings about the dangers of inaction.

2) What assumptions are being made by the critics of environmental policies?
The critics assume that the cost of green energy outweighs the potential damage caused by climate change.

3) How does the author balance the opposing viewpoints?
The author gives space to both sides but needs more detailed evidence for both arguments.

4) Are there any logical fallacies present in the argument?
The editorial may suffer from a false balance fallacy—presenting both sides equally, even if one has more scientific backing.

5) What further questions do you have after reading this editorial?
What are the specific economic impacts of green energy policies?
What evidence exists to support the claim that climate change is exaggerated?

Write a Reflection on a Chosen Article or Book Chapter:

Instructions:
- Choose an article or a chapter from a book that resonates with you.
- Write a 250-word reflection where you:
  - Summarize the main points
  - Connect the text with your own life experiences
  - Identify any biases or assumptions present in the text
  - Please share what you learned from reading it

Example Reflection: "I read an article about the effects of social media on teens. It made me think about my habits and time spent online. The author's point about social media affecting sleep patterns resonated with me because I've experienced that myself. The author assumed that all teens use social media similarly, which isn't true for everyone. The article made me realize I need to rethink how I use my screen time."

Additional Tips for Critical Reading:

- **Take Notes:** Jot down key points, thoughts, and questions as you read. This can help clarify your thinking and keep you engaged.
- **Discuss with Others:** Engage in conversations with classmates or teachers. Discussing your ideas will help refine your thoughts and lead to new insights.
- **Practice Regularly:** Like any skill, critical reading gets better with practice. Make a habit of engaging deeply with different kinds of texts.

By using critical thinking strategies, high school students can develop into more insightful and creative readers, improving comprehension and essential skills for growth.

Trivia Corner

Reading with a Critical Eye

- **Socratic questioning: A technique used to encourage critical thinking by asking probing questions.**
  - Example: Socrates famously used this method to challenge his students' assumptions about knowledge and morality. He would ask questions like, "What is justice?" and "What is the nature of good?" to guide them toward a more profound understanding.

- **Fallacies: Common errors in reasoning that can undermine critical thinking.**
  - Example: A common fallacy is the ad hominem attack, in which someone attacks the person making an argument rather than addressing the argument itself. This can be seen in political debates, where opponents insult each other instead of discussing the issues.

- **Bias: A prejudice or inclination that can influence one's judgment.**
  - Example: During the Cold War, many people in the United States had a strong bias against communism, influencing their interpretation of news and events related to the Soviet Union.

Asking Deeper Questions

- **Wh-questions: Who, what, when, where, why, and how questions can encourage more profound analysis.**
  - Example: When reading a historical document, asking questions like "Who wrote this?" and "When was it written?" can help you understand the context and the author's perspective.

- **Open-ended questions require more than a simple yes or no answer.**
  - Example: Instead of asking, "Did you like the book?" you could ask, "What did you think about the main character's actions?" to encourage a more thoughtful response.

- **Metacognition: Thinking about one's thinking processes.**
  - Example: After reading an article, you might ask yourself, "What did I learn from this?" and "How does this information relate to what I already know?" to reflect on your understanding.

TRIVIA CORNER

Reflecting on the Text: Connecting with Personal Experiences

Personal connections: Relating the text to one's own life or experiences.

- Example: While reading a novel about a character facing a difficult decision, you might think about a similar situation you've experienced and how you handled it.

Empathy: Understanding and sharing the feelings of others.

- Example: When reading a memoir about someone's struggles with mental health, you might try to put yourself in their shoes and imagine how they must have felt.

Perspective-taking: Considering different viewpoints.

- Example: After reading a news article about a controversial issue, you might try to understand people's arguments on both sides of the debate.

Trivia: How critical thinking impacts decision-making skills

Informed decision-making: Critical thinking helps individuals make well-informed choices by evaluating information and considering potential consequences.

- Example: Critical thinking can help you weigh the pros and cons of different options, consider your long-term goals, and decide which college to attend.

Trivia: How critical thinking impacts decision-making skills

Informed decision-making: Critical thinking helps individuals make well-informed choices by evaluating information and considering potential consequences.

- Example: When deciding which college to attend, critical thinking can help you weigh the pros and cons of different options, consider your long-term goals, and make an informed decision.

🎯 ACTIVITY CORNER 9

Activity 1: Match the Author's Intent

Instructions: Match the following passages to the author's intent: Persuade, Inform, or Entertain.

Passages:

1. A newspaper article discussing the benefits of a plant-based diet.
2. It is a fantasy short story about a young wizard saving his kingdom.
3. An informative report on how climate change affects polar bears.
4. A commercial script promoting a new smartphone.
5. A blog post encouraging people to vote in the upcoming election.

Activity 2: True or False: Critical Thinking in Action

Instructions: Read the statements below and determine if they are True or False based on the chapter's content.

1. Critical thinking only applies to academic texts.
2. Reflective reading helps you connect a text to your own life experiences.
3. Bias in a text can only be detected if it's overt.
4. Asking deeper questions leads to a more thorough understanding of the material.
5. Critical reading helps improve empathy.

Activity 3: Identify Bias and Assumptions

Instructions: Read the short passage and identify any bias or assumptions the author may have.

Passage:

- "Video games are a waste of time. Instead of playing games, kids should be outside in nature, engaging in physical activity. All video games do is promote violence and laziness."

🎯 ACTIVITY CORNER 9

Questions:

1. What is the author's bias?
2. What assumption is the author making?
3. Is there any evidence provided to support these claims?

Activity 4: Tone and Bias Quiz

Instructions: Read the following passages and determine the author's tone (Positive, Negative, Neutral) and if there is any bias.

Passage:

- "The new government policy on education is a step forward, showing how much the administration cares about our children's future."

- "The policy is a joke, doing nothing but waste taxpayer money on ineffective programs."

- "The policy proposes changes to the education system, including more funding for schools in low-income areas."

- "Our politicians only care about getting votes; their policies are just smoke and mirrors."

- "The program aims to improve education standards but has received mixed reviews from educators."

10. Mastering Reading Comprehension for Exams: SAT, ACT, and Beyond

Understanding what you read is crucial for tests like the SAT and ACT. This chapter explains the test format, strategies for different questions, and helpful tips for high school students. Acquiring the necessary skills to tackle these sections effectively can improve your performance.

Understanding the Exam Format

Overview of SAT and ACT Reading Sections

The SAT and ACT have dedicated reading sections that assess your ability to understand written passages across various subjects such as literature, history, science, and social studies. Here's a breakdown:

Exam	Number of Passages	Number of Questions	Time Allotted
SAT	5 Passages	52 Questions	65 Minutes
ACT	4 Passages	40 Questions	35 Minutes

Time Constraints and Question Types

Both exams pose time challenges. The SAT allows about 75 seconds per question, while the ACT allows around 53 seconds per question. Effective time management is crucial to avoid rushing through questions.

- **Types of Passages**: Fictional excerpts, historical documents, science articles, and social studies essays.
- **Question Types:** Multiple choice, asking about main ideas, details, inferences, vocabulary in context, tone, and the function of sentences.

Practical Example: SAT Reading Breakdown

Here's a sample SAT passage excerpt from a science article about environmental conservation.

"Recent studies reveal that urban green spaces can improve air quality, reduce stress levels, and provide habitats for local wildlife. These findings have prompted cities to increase their investment in parks and green roofs, particularly in areas with high population density."

Sample Question:

What is the primary purpose of the passage?

- A) To discuss the importance of wildlife preservation
- B) To explain how urban green spaces benefit the environment
- C) To criticize cities for not doing enough
- D) To suggest ways individuals can contribute to environmental conservation

Answer: B) To explain how urban green spaces benefit the environment

Exercise:

Familiarize yourself with the timing of passages by timing yourself while reading a passage. Set a timer for 2 minutes and see how much of the passage you can read while retaining key points.

Types of Reading Comprehension Questions

Question Type	What It Tests	Strategy
Main Idea/Primary Purpose	Understanding the overall point	Focus on topic sentences and conclusions
Detail	Specific facts or information	Scan the passage for keywords
Inference	Reading between the lines	Use evidence from the text
Vocabulary in Context	Meaning of words in the passage	Rely on context clues
Function	Purpose of a sentence or paragraph	Think about why the author included it
Tone and Attitude	Author's mood or attitude toward topic	Analyze word choice and phrasing

Exercise:

Read the following passage excerpt:

"Scientists have long debated the reasons behind the decline in honeybee populations. While some attribute the drop to pesticides, others believe climate change is the main culprit."

Identify the question types for the following questions:

1. What is the main idea of the passage? (Main Idea Question)
2. According to the passage, what factors might cause the decline in honeybee populations? (Detail Question)
3. The word "culprit" most likely means...? (Vocabulary in Context)

Approaching the Passage: Quick Strategies

Skimming vs. Careful Reading: When to Use Each

- **Skimming**: Useful for passages with lots of detail. Focus on topic sentences, paragraphs' first and last sentences, and any headings.

- **Careful Reading:** Necessary for more complex or abstract passages, such as those from literature or philosophy.

The 'First Sentence' Trick

The first sentence of each paragraph often contains the main idea. Skimming through these can help you quickly identify the overall structure and purpose of the passage.

Reading the Questions First
Before you dive into the passage, please read the questions. This will give you an idea of what to look for as you read, allowing you to focus on specific text parts.

Practical Example: Applying Skimming
Take this excerpt:

"The rapid expansion of digital media has changed how people consume information. While newspapers and magazines once monopolized news, social media platforms have become the dominant source of information for many."

Skim for Key Points:

- First sentence: Main idea about digital media and its impact.
- Keywords: "rapid expansion," "social media," "dominant source."

Exercise:

Practice skimming the passage and answering the main idea question. Set a timer for 30 seconds and try to summarize the key points.

Tackling Each Question Type Efficiently

Question Type	Strategy	Example
Main Idea	Use topic sentences and conclusion clues	Question: What is the passage about?
Detail	Find and match keywords from passage to question	Question: According to the passage, how do green spaces help?
Inference	Use logic based on textual evidence	Question: What can be inferred about the author's opinion?
Vocabulary in Context	Focus on surrounding words to deduce meaning	Question: What does "culprit" most likely mean?
Function	Consider the purpose of a sentence/paragraph	Question: Why does the author mention green roofs?

Practical Example: Tackling an Inference Question

Question: What can be inferred about the author's view on urban green spaces?

Answer: The author views green spaces as beneficial to both the environment and people's well-being, as indicated by the positive outcomes (improving air quality and reducing stress).

Exercise:

- Answer the following SAT/ACT-style questions based on the passage provided earlier. For each, identify the type of question and apply the appropriate strategy.

Questions :

1. What is the main idea of the passage? (Main Idea)
2. According to the passage, what do green roofs provide for wildlife? (Detail)
3. The author implies that cities should… (Inference)
4. What does the word "investment" mean in this context? (Vocabulary in Context)
5. Why does the author include the findings from recent studies? (Function)

Answers:

1. *Main Idea: The benefits of urban green spaces*
2. *Detail: Habitats for local wildlife*
3. *Inference: Continue to increase their investment in green spaces*
4. *Vocabulary in Context: Commitment of resources for future benefit*
5. *Function: To support the argument that urban green spaces are beneficial*

By mastering these strategies, practicing regularly, and developing strong comprehension skills, you'll be better prepared for the SAT, ACT, and beyond!

Trivia Corner

- *Passage-Based Focus:* The SAT reading section now exclusively features passage-based reading comprehension questions, eliminating sentence completion questions.

- *Time Management:* While the average time spent on each ACT reading question is around 53 seconds, effective time management strategies are crucial for success.

- *Skimming and Careful Reading:* Skimming can provide a general overview, but careful reading of key details and evidence is essential for accurate comprehension.
- *Question Preview:* Reviewing questions before reading the passage can help you focus on relevant information and improve your comprehension.
- *Paragraph Structure:* The first and last sentences of a paragraph often contain the main idea, providing valuable clues for summarizing.
- *Vocabulary in Context:* Understanding word usage in context is crucial, as vocabulary questions typically make up 15-20% of the SAT and ACT reading sections.
- *Scientific Focus:* The ACT reading section includes a passage specifically focused on natural sciences, making familiarity with scientific terminology beneficial.
- *Author's Tone and Purpose:* Actively identifying the author's tone and purpose can significantly improve your reading comprehension scores.
- *Summarization:* Summarizing a passage in your own words after reading it can enhance retention and understanding.
- *Diverse Topics:* Both the SAT and ACT reading sections cover a variety of topics, including literature, social science, and science passages. Broad reading can help you prepare for different types of questions.

ACTIVITY CORNER 10

Activity 1: Main Idea/Primary Purpose Questions

Instructions: Determine the main idea or primary purpose in the following passage.

Passage:

"Technology is rapidly changing our world, making life easier in countless ways. Technological advancements transform communication, work, and thinking from smartphones to artificial intelligence. However, the rise of technology comes with challenges, such as privacy concerns and the potential for job loss due to automation."

Question:

What is the primary purpose of the passage?

1. To warn about the dangers of technology.
2. To explore how technology impacts privacy.
3. To discuss both the benefits and challenges of technological advancements.
4. To highlight how technology has changed communication.

Activity 2: Detail Questions

Instructions: Please read the following passage and answer the detailed question based on specific information.

Passage:

"In the rainforest, species diversity is one of the most remarkable aspects of the ecosystem. For example, in a single hectare, scientists have documented hundreds of different species of plants, animals, and insects. This variety is crucial for the health and stability of the environment."

Question:

According to the passage, why is biodiversity in the rainforest important?

1. It ensures the survival of endangered species.
2. It is necessary for the health and stability of the environment.
3. It helps scientists discover new species.
4. It increases the beauty of the rainforest.

ACTIVITY CORNER 10

Activity 3: Inference Questions

Instructions: Read the passage below and answer the inference question.

Passage:

"John stared at the job offer in his hand. The salary was great, the location was ideal, yet something nagged at him. It was the long hours and the uncertainty of the company's future that gave him pause. Still, he knew that opportunities like this didn't come often."

Question:

What can be inferred about John's feelings toward the job offer?

1. He is excited and ready to accept the offer immediately.
2. He is hesitant and unsure about accepting due to concerns about the company's stability.
3. He is indifferent and believes other offers will come along.
4. He is disappointed by the salary being too low.

Activity 4: Vocabulary in Context Questions

Instructions: Use context clues to determine the meaning of the highlighted word.

Passage:

"The politician's speech was a calculated ploy to win over undecided voters. Despite its polished delivery, many saw through the ploy and were unimpressed by the empty promises."

Question:

What is the meaning of the word ploy in this context?

1. Genuine statement
2. Insincere effort
3. Logical argument
4. Honest mistake

ACTIVITY CORNER 10

Activity 5: Function Questions

Instructions: Read the passage and answer the function question about the role of a sentence or paragraph.

Passage:

"Environmental concerns have pushed for more sustainable farming practices in recent years. Some farms have adopted new techniques such as crop rotation and organic fertilization. These methods help the environment and improve crop yields over time."

Question:

What is the passage's function of the sentence "These methods not only help the environment but also improve crop yields over time"?

1. To introduce a new idea unrelated to farming.
2. To support the argument that sustainable farming practices are beneficial.
3. To criticize traditional farming methods.
4. To explain the drawbacks of organic fertilization.

Activity 6: Author's Tone and Attitude Questions

Instructions: Read the following passage and determine the author's tone and attitude toward the subject.

Passage:

"In today's fast-paced world, it is easy to overlook the importance of taking time for self-care. While society tends to celebrate constant productivity and hustle, few recognize the burnout that follows. It's essential to prioritize rest and mental well-being to lead a fulfilling life, yet this is often dismissed as laziness by those who value work above all else."

Question:

What is the author's tone and attitude toward the concept of self-care?

1. Critical and dismissive
2. Supportive and advocating
3. Neutral and objective
4. Skeptical and questioning

ACTIVITY ANSWERS

ACTIVITY CORNER 1

1. **Identify the Reading Type**

   1. Non-Fiction
   2. Fiction
   3. Technical
   4. Literary
   5. Non-Fiction

2. **Match the Reading Purpose**

   1. 1 → d
   2. 2 → c
   3. 3 → a
   4. 4 → b

ACTIVITY CORNER 2

1) Activity Exercise: Main Idea Matching

Answers:
- Main Idea A: Recycling helps reduce waste in landfills. → Supporting Detail 2
- Main Idea B: Regular sleep improves memory and focus. → Supporting Detail 1
- Main Idea C: Eating fruits and vegetables promotes a healthy lifestyle. → Supporting Detail 3

2) Main Idea Identification Quiz

Passage 1:
Answer: The internet has revolutionized communication by allowing instant global connections.

Passage 2:
Answer: Regular exercise improves physical health.

3) Find the Main Idea in a News Article

Answer: Urban green spaces help reduce air pollution in cities.

ACTIVITY CORNER 3

EXERCISE 1: TRUE OR FALSE - SUPPORTING DETAILS

Answers:
1. True
2. False
3. True
4. True
5. False

EXERCISE 2: MAIN IDEA AND SUPPORTING DETAILS MATCH

- Answers:
    a. Main Idea A → Detail 2
    b. Main Idea B → Detail 3
    c. Main Idea C → Detail 1

EXERCISE 3: PASSAGE ANNOTATION

Answers:
- Solar energy reduces reliance on fossil fuels, a major carbon emission source.
- Wind power provides a clean, renewable alternative to coal and natural gas.
- Wind power can be generated on a large scale without contributing to air pollution.

EXERCISE 4: FILL IN THE GAPS

Answers:

a) **Education** helps individuals gain the skills needed to find better-paying jobs.
b) Studies have shown that **higher education** leads to improved economic outcomes for entire communities.
c) Access to **quality education** increases opportunities for social mobility and personal growth

ACTIVITY CORNER 4

ACTIVITY 1: INFERRING CHARACTER MOTIVES :

Answer Key:
1. She may be avoiding the person calling her.
2. She is likely feeling nervous or worried.
3. She might be concerned about someone following or watching her.
4. She could be under time pressure or concerned about being late for something important.
5. She may have a complicated or tense relationship with the caller.

ACTIVITY 2: INFERRING FROM DIALOGUE :

Answer Key:
1. Sarah is upset and feels betrayed.
2. Mark might have broken a promise or done something against Sarah's wishes.
3. Mark feels regretful but believes his actions were justified.
4. They have a close relationship, but trust has been compromised.
5. The situation was likely out of Mark's control, leading to his actions.

ACTIVITY 3: INFERENCES FROM CONTEXT CLUES :

Answer Key:
1. Dilapidated likely means run-down or in a state of disrepair.
2. Facade refers to the front or exterior of the house, likely implying it was once beautiful.
3. Maleficent suggests something evil or harmful, enhancing the eerie atmosphere of the story.
4. The townspeople are scared and superstitious, avoiding the house due to its reputation.
5. The passage's tone is ominous and foreboding, suggesting danger or mystery.

ACTIVITY CORNER 5

Activity 1: Author's Purpose Quiz (Multiple Choice)

1. Answer: B. Persuade
2. Answer: A. Inform
3. Answer: C. Entertain
4. Answer: C. Inspire
5. Answer: A. Inform

Activity 2: Match the Tone with the Passage

Answer Key:
1. Joyful
2. Angry
3. Calm
4. Reflective
5. Sarcastic

Activity 3: Multiple Choice (Identify the Tone)

1. Answer: B. Angry
2. Answer: B. Thrilling
3. Answer: A. Anxious
4. Answer: C. Joyful
5. Answer: A. Neutral

Activity 4: Match the Following (Author's Purpose)

Answer Key:

1. Persuade
2. Inform
3. Entertain
4. Inspire

ACTIVITY CORNER 6

ACTIVITY 1: MATCH THE WORD WITH ITS DEFINITION

Answers:
1 - C, 2 - D, 3 - A, 4 - B, 5 - E

ACTIVITY 2: TRUE OR FALSE - VOCABULARY IN CONTEXT

1. False
2. False
3. True
4. False
5. False

ACTIVITY 3: MULTIPLE CHOICE - CONTEXT CLUES

1. Answer: B. Sharp, insightful
2. Answer: A. Unbelievable
3. Answer: B. Complicated, twisted
4. Answer: A. Calm and peaceful
5. Answer: B. Perfect, without fault

ACTIVITY CORNER 7

ACTIVITY 1: MATCH THE STRUCTURE

Answer Key:

1. Chronological
2. Cause and Effect
3. Compare and Contrast
4. Problem and Solution
5. Cause and Effect

ACTIVITY 2: TRUE OR FALSE

Answer Key:

1. False
2. True
3. False
4. False
5. True

ACTIVITY CORNER 7

ACTIVITY 3 : IDENTIFY THE STRUCTURE

Answers:

1. Problem and Solution
2. Chronological
3. Cause and Effect

ACTIVITY 4 : TEXT STRUCTURE SORTING

Answer Key:

1. Cause and Effect: Passage 1
2. Compare and Contrast: Passage 2
3. Chronological: Passage 5
4. Problem and Solution: Passage 4

ACTIVITY CORNER 8

ACTIVITY 1: MATCH THE PARAPHRASES

Answer:
1. A
2. B
3. C

ACTIVITY 2 : TRUE OR FALSE - SUMMARIZING

Answer:
1. False
2. False
3. True
4. False
5. True

ACTIVITY 3 : MATCH THE AUTHOR'S PURPOSE

Answer:
1. A
2. B
3. C
4. B
5. A

ACTIVITY 4 : IDENTIFY THE MAIN IDEA AND SUMMARIZE

Main Idea: AI is advancing across multiple industries, but it also presents ethical concerns.

Summary: Artificial Intelligence is making significant advancements in fields like healthcare and finance, but it also raises important ethical issues related to privacy and security.

ACTIVITY CORNER 9

ACTIVITY 1 : MATCH THE AUTHOR'S INTENT

Answers:

1. Persuade
2. Entertain
3. Inform
4. Persuade
5. Persuade

ACTIVITY 2 : TRUE OR FALSE: CRITICAL THINKING IN ACTION

Answers:

1. False
2. True
3. False
4. True
5. True

ACTIVITY 3 : IDENTIFY BIAS AND ASSUMPTIONS

Answers:

1. The author is biased against video games and believes they have negative impacts.
2. The author assumes that all video games promote violence and that kids should spend all their free time outdoors.
3. No evidence is provided to support the claims made.

ACTIVITY 4 : TONE AND BIAS QUIZ

Answers:

1. Positive, bias towards the government.
2. Negative, bias against the policy.
3. Neutral, no clear bias.
4. Negative, bias against politicians.
5. Neutral, acknowledges both sides.

ACTIVITY CORNER 10

ACTIVITY 1 (MAIN IDEA/PRIMARY PURPOSE):
- Answer: 3. To discuss both the benefits and challenges of technological advancements.

ACTIVITY 2 (DETAIL QUESTION):
- Answer: 2. It is necessary for the health and stability of the environment.

ACTIVITY 3 (INFERENCE QUESTION):
- Answer: 2. He is hesitant and unsure about accepting due to concerns about the company's stability.

ACTIVITY 4 (VOCABULARY IN CONTEXT QUESTION):
- Answer: 2. Insincere effort

ACTIVITY 5 (FUNCTION QUESTION):
- Answer: 2. To support the argument that sustainable farming practices are beneficial.

ACTIVITY 6 (AUTHOR'S TONE AND ATTITUDE QUESTIONS):
- Answer: 2. Supportive and advocating

Please let us know how we're doing by leaving us a review.

CONCLUSION: YOUR JOURNEY TO MASTERING READING COMPREHENSION

Congratulations! You've completed Reading Comprehension High School: Reading Comprehension Grades 9-12 Workbook. By now, you've gained a deeper understanding of what it takes to become a confident, skillful reader—whether for standardized exams like the SAT and ACT, school assignments, or personal growth.

Key Takeaways:

- **Understanding the Fundamentals:** From recognizing the main idea to identifying supporting details and making inferences, you've mastered the essential building blocks of reading comprehension. These skills are foundational, not just for exams, but for critical thinking and communication in everyday life.

- **Adapting to Various Texts**: You've learned how to approach different types of texts—from fiction and non-fiction to technical documents and literary passages. This versatility will help you excel in school, career, and beyond.

- **Strategic Reading for Exams:** With tips on time management, question types, and test-taking strategies, you're better prepared to tackle the reading sections of the SAT, ACT, and other standardized tests. You know how to approach passages, analyze questions, and apply specific strategies to find answers.

- **Applying Your Skills in Real Life**: The reading skills you've developed are not just academic—they have real-world applications. Whether interpreting information at work, reflecting on articles, or navigating the digital age with AI outputs, reading comprehension is a lifelong skill that will help you succeed in all areas of life.

CONCLUSION: YOUR JOURNEY TO MASTERING READING COMPREHENSION

Moving Forward:

- Practice Makes Perfect: Continue applying the strategies and exercises you've learned in this workbook. The more you practice, the more comfortable you become with complex texts and challenging questions.

- Stay Curious: Keep reading widely. Dive into different genres, explore new topics, and challenge yourself with materials outside your comfort zone. Reading comprehension is a skill that grows with each new page you turn.

- Reflect and Connect: Make it a habit to read and think critically about what you read. Ask questions, make inferences, and reflect on how the text connects to your life and experiences.

Final Words of Encouragement:

Reading is more than a skill; it's a gateway to understanding the world. The techniques you've learned here are stepping stones to becoming a better reader, whether for pleasure, study, or work. Remember, every great reader was once a beginner. Keep honing your skills; you'll see how far they can take you.

Good luck on your reading journey and beyond!

APPENDIX -A :
COMMON READING COMPREHENSION STRATEGIES

Common Reading Comprehension Strategies

Strategy	Description	Purpose	Example Application
Skimming	Quickly reading a passage to get the main idea	To get a general overview of the text	Skim the introduction and conclusion of an article
Scanning	Looking for specific information or keywords	To locate details or answers quickly	Scan a passage for dates or names in a history text
Annotating	Making notes or highlighting important sections	To engage with the text and identify key points	Underline important quotes in a novel
Summarizing	Restating the main points in your own words	To check understanding and condense information	Summarize a paragraph after reading
Making Inferences	Drawing conclusions based on evidence in the text	To understand implied meanings and deepen comprehension	Infer the meaning of a character's actions in a story

Applying Reading Strategies to Different Types of Passages

Passage Type	Best Strategy to Apply	Example Application
Fictional Short Story	Annotating and Summarizing	Highlight key moments and summarize character development
Scientific Article	Scanning and Inferences	Scan for relevant data points, infer the implications of findings
Historical Document	Skimming and Annotating	Skim for the main argument, annotate significant dates and events
Opinion Editorial	Critical Reading and Inferences	Infer the author's bias and assess the strength of their argument

APPENDIX -B :
READING COMPREHENSION QUESTION TYPES

Breakdown of Reading Comprehension Question Types

Question Type	Definition	Common Focus Points
Main Idea	Identifying the central message of the passage	What is the passage primarily about?
Supporting Details	Locating facts and evidence that support the main idea	What evidence does the author provide?
Inference	Drawing logical conclusions based on the text	What can be inferred but not directly stated?
Vocabulary in Context	Determining the meaning of a word based on surrounding text	What does the word mean in this context?
Author's Purpose	Understanding the reason for writing the passage	Why did the author write this text?

Sample Questions by Type with Tips on How to Find the Answer

Question Type	Sample Generic Question	Tips on How to Find the Answer
Main Idea	What is the main idea of the passage?	Tip: Look at the first and last sentences of the passage for clues. Identify recurring themes or ideas that are discussed throughout the text. The main idea typically summarizes the central argument or purpose of the text.
Supporting Details	Which detail supports the author's main argument?	Tip: Locate sentences or phrases that provide evidence, examples, or explanations directly related to the main argument. Supporting details often reinforce the central point and are usually specific facts, statistics, or anecdotes.
Inference	What can be inferred from the passage?	Tip: Read between the lines. Consider what is implied but not directly stated. Inferences are often derived from the tone, context, and underlying messages of the text. Use logical reasoning based on the given information.
Vocabulary in Context	What does the word "resilient" most likely mean in this context?	Tip: Look at the surrounding words and sentences to understand how the word is used. Identify synonyms or phrases nearby that could hint at the meaning. Pay attention to the overall tone or mood to determine if the word has a positive, negative, or neutral connotation.
Author's Purpose	What is the author's primary purpose in writing the passage?	Tip: Consider the tone of the passage (informative, persuasive, or entertaining). Is the author trying to educate, convince, or tell a story? Look for direct statements of intent, or analyze the subject matter and how the author approaches it.

APPENDIX -C :
TIPS FOR TEST-TAKING

Time Management Tips

Tip	Explanation
Prioritize easier questions	Answer easy questions first to save time
Set mini-goals during the test	Allocate specific minutes per section
Skim the passage first	Get a general sense before diving into questions

Strategies for Overcoming Test Anxiety

Strategy	Description
Breathing Exercises	Practice deep breathing before and during the test
Positive Visualization	Picture yourself succeeding to build confidence

APPENDIX - D :
GLOSSARY OF READING COMPREHENSION TERMS

Key Terms

Term	Definition	Example
Inference	A conclusion drawn from evidence and reasoning	From the author's tone, we infer they are concerned about climate change.
Main Idea	The central concept of a passage	The main idea of the passage is the importance of renewable energy.
Context Clues	Hints within the text that help define unfamiliar words	The word "elated" means happy, as seen from the joyful context.

APPENDIX - E :
COMMON READING COMPREHENSION ERRORS

Common Mistakes & Tips for Avoiding Errors

Error	Description	Solution
Misreading the main idea	Focusing on details without grasping the overall message	Summarize the passage after reading
Ignoring context clues	Misunderstanding a word by ignoring surrounding words	Practice identifying co

Tip	Explanation
Always refer back to the passage	Revisit the text to confirm your answers
Read the questions carefully	Ensure you understand what each question is asking

YOUNG WRITER SERIES - DR. FANATOMY

We'd Love Your Feedback!

★ ★ ★ ★ ★

Please let us know how we're doing by leaving us a review.

www.ingramcontent.com/pod-product-compliance
Lightning Source LLC
Chambersburg PA
CBHW082211070526
44585CB00020B/2373